ON TRACK
for a life of excellence

Coach Chick Hislop

On Track

Published by Fast Track Publisher
Ogden, Utah

Cover and Text Design: Eric Barkle / ebarkle@me.com / 801-368-0876

Creative Editor: Thomas Cantrell / Tom@TomCantrell.com / 801-355-2005

Edit Team: Brad Barton; Su Boddie; Jill Gibson; Dianne, Chris, Lance, and Teresa Hislop; Rich Hopkins; Mark Housley; Kathie Leany; Kim Meikle; Mike and Kristie Spence

Dedicated to my student athletes
who taught me so much...

...and to my wife
who gently reminds me
how much I still need to learn!

Acknowledgments

There are only fifteen stories in this book, involving maybe forty athletes and coaches I've worked with. I've loved and learned from them all and from hundreds of others.

I didn't always realize how great they were at the time I was with them. As time passed, it became evident how inspiring they were as individuals and what great examples they were to me.

To name all of these wonderful student athletes and coaches, along with all the family and friends who helped create this book, would require a whole 'nother book. I guess I better get started on the second volume.

TABLE OF CONTENTS

Prologue

Brad Barton, NCAA All-American distance runner
American and International champion
Masters Track World record holder

The finest coaches in the world are coaches who *never stop asking questions*.

Whether novice, experienced or seasoned veterans, no matter what status they have attained in their careers, they continue to ask questions. They seek, learn, invent and reinvent.

These coaches are always students. They know that mentors need mentors, coaches need coaches. This regrettably rare breed continuously strives to jettison their mediocrity-inducing pride. These teachers perpetually search for ways to step humbly into the role of student.

They know that everyone with whom they come in contact is potentially a guide. They seek coaches to coach them on being better coaches – better people. These outstanding coaches *are always asking questions – always learning.*

Such is USA Track and Field Hall of Fame and Olympic Coach, Chick Hislop. When we learn from this kind of coach, we are not just getting his opinion; we are getting the distilled knowledge of all the wonderful teachers and mentors whose direction he has sought out.

His guidance has redirected my path on many occasions; not just on the track, but getting back on track in every area of my life. With all my love and respect, dear reader, I give you Coach Chick Hislop. I hope you enjoy his book as much as I appreciate and value him.

1

Skinny Billy

Raise the Bar

Throw your heart over the bar and your body will follow.
  ~ *Anonymous*

The secret of getting ahead is getting started. The secret of getting started is breaking your complex overwhelming tasks into small manageable tasks, and starting on the first one.
  ~ *Mark Twain*

It is fine to aim high if we have developed the ability to accomplish our aims, but there is no use aiming unless the gun is loaded.
  ~ *William Ross*

It is not a disgrace not to reach the stars, but it is a disgrace to have no stars to reach for. Not failure, but low aim is a sin.
  ~ *Benjamin E. Mays*

Goal-setting *seems* easy, but it's generally not. For most of us, most of the time, it's difficult to decide and even more difficult to follow through on our plans. To say boldly you are going to do something is one thing: "I am going to win a state championship," "I will be the best in the region," "I'll be the top earner this year."

To actually achieve something, however, is quite another thing.

The difficulty is to get clear and specific. It is important that you set your objective in concrete detailed steps with the procedures and plans, and the vision and words which inspire you to achieve your personal best. Then use that vision to inspire deep determination and commitment within you.

Then do it.
Then do it again.
Then again…until you get it right.

And most important of all?
Ya gotta' have heart.

Having heart empowers you to see past adversity with the will to do things you have never done before – perhaps something *no one* has ever done before. Having heart is the key to victory. You may replace one goal setting model with another but there is no replacing "heart" in the equation.

My first coaching job (1961) was as a track & field coach at Ben Lomond High School in Ogden, Utah. I was young – just two years out of college. I wanted to be successful, of course. I had great goals, but I really didn't understand how to take the steps to reach them. At Ben Lomond, I had the privilege of coaching two outstanding young men who inadvertently taught *me* a lot about goal setting.

The best teachers are always students. The best coaches are always looking for better ways of doing things. They are always willing and eager to learn from anyone – whether that person is trying to teach them or not.

From my student athletes' examples, I learned how to successfully follow the steps and procedures toward achieving *my* goals. As I watched them set and achieve their own goals, I came to realize what it meant to be a true goal setter.

The first of these two young men was nicknamed "Skinny Billy."

He stood 6'6" and weighed less than one hundred and forty pounds. Billy was the class clown. Actually, he was the *school* clown. If anything fun or funny happened, you could bet that Billy was in the middle of it.

Ben Lomond was a new school – only five years old – but already rich with tradition. We were the Ben Lomond Scots. Our tradition was to get a student to wear a kilt[1] on game day.

Billy volunteered to wear the kilt. Remember, this was long before it was fashionable for a man to wear a skirt! You can only imagine how this tall, thin kid looked and acted in a colorful, traditional, and fairly short kilt.

Every game day, for every sports activity during the year, Billy wore the kilt. There was much enthusiastic hooting and hollering. You could tell when Billy was on the move because the volume would go up as he walked down the hall.

Interestingly, as soon as he walked into a classroom, and the bell rang, the silliness stopped. It was as if he became a different person. He did not goof around during class time. He was a senior with a 4.0 GPA, very goal oriented and serious about his school work.

As soon as the bell would ring to end the class, however, he once again became the jovial school clown – in a kilt.

Billy was also an aspiring athlete – a high jumper. Despite his height, though, he was not very good. When I got the coaching job at Ben Lomond, he approached me.

"So, you're the new coach!"

---

1   "A kilt is a short traditional skirt worn by men in Scotland. Although the kilt is most often worn on formal occasions and at Highland games and sports events, it has also been adapted as an item of informal male clothing in recent years, returning to its roots as an everyday garment." https://en.wikipedia.org/wiki/Kilt

"Yes. That's right."

"I want to win the state championship in the high jump. Can you help me do that?"

"Oh boy! That's great, Bill. How high can you jump?"

"Six feet."

I wasn't impressed, but I tried to be nice.

"Well, Bill, six feet certainly won't win a state championship. Do you know what you have to do to win the championship?"

"Yes. Wait a minute, Coach." He popped opened his notebook, took out a piece of paper and handed it to me. I was startled at the detail of plan and the thoroughness of the goals he had set to prepare himself to win a state championship that year.

Now, I *was* impressed!

High on his list of objectives was to improve his overall strength through weight lifting.

"I need your help with this," he said. "I know I've got to get stronger, but I don't know what weights I'm supposed to use."

The school did not have a weight room, much less a weight training program, so we improvised. Together we created a plan that would help him achieve his objectives.

Also on his list was a plan to specifically enhance his jumping ability. He had listed several activities he thought would enhance his leg strength. One of them was running.

The problem was, we did not have a winter track program. So, again, he innovated. He decided to develop his jumping skills and the explosive power necessary to achieve greater jumping heights by playing basketball.

I told him that was a good plan.

He had an even better plan. He wasn't satisfied with joining just one team; he signed up for three different leagues!

It's hard to keep up with a motivated, goal-oriented athlete!

As the year went on, and I got better acquainted with Billy, I asked him what he was planned to do after he graduated.

Without hesitation he startled me with a clearly stated and rather ambitious goal. "I am going to be a heart surgeon."

He didn't say "I *want* to be a *doctor*." He was laser specific. "I am *going* to be a *heart surgeon*."

I thought, "How could this ever happen?" His father had been killed in the Korean War. His family finances were limited. His mother worked full time to support him and his brother.

But, still, his confident declaration echoed in my heart. "I'm *going* to college. I'm *going* to be a *heart surgeon*."

"How do you plan to go to college?" I carefully asked.

His answer was as specific as was his goal. "I will earn an academic scholarship and I will win a track scholarship. I will work part time during my first four years in college and save up for medical school."

His response really got my attention. This young man knew as much about goal setting as any successful adult. The student was, indeed, the teacher.

As the season progressed, Billy made remarkable progress. He proved to be a determined competitor. He won the regional championship, clearing the bar at 6'3" – his personal best. With that, I thought he might just have a chance to *place* in the state meet, because though 6'3" was his best, it certainly wasn't good enough to win the championship.

He went into the state competition ranked below the top six. The prognosis wasn't good.

This was before the Fosbury Flop was developed by Dick Fosbury, the 1964 High Jump Olympic Gold Medalist. All the jumpers still used the Western Roll, a technique where the jumper's entire body cleared the bar at the same time. This technique was limiting. It made it very difficult to achieve a significant height.

At the state meet, Billy was the happiest guy on the team. Why? Because the day was cold and windy and he was certain the inclement weather would psych-out his competition.

He was right. Some of the higher-ranked jumpers had missed at some of the lower heights. Billy cleared the bar at 6'3" – equal to his all-time best – but he did it without a miss at any previous height. They moved the bar to 6'4" and he made it on his first attempt. He then cleared 6'5" – again without a miss.

The weather grew worse with increasing wind and chilling rain. Other jumpers who had gone higher than Billy before this competition started to miss. The poor weather conditions, however, only spurred Billy on.

The bar was raised to 6'6". Billy turned to me and said, "If I can make this one on my first attempt, without a miss, I will be the state champion because no one will make 6'7" in these conditions." It was uncommon for a young athlete to have such deep understanding of strategy in what most people would consider a physical contest.

All he had to do was break his own personal record three times in one day! That was quite a feat – but that was his goal. He stood quiet and still at the beginning of his approach, visualizing his run-up, takeoff, and bar clearance. You could see his focus and determination. He overstepped his approach and grazed the bar. It vibrated and bounced. Miraculously, it stayed on. He made 6'6!" – setting his third personal record in one day!

Two other jumpers also made 6'6", but they had misses at lower heights. As the bar was moved to 6'7" the skies opened and cold rain came pouring down. No one made 6'7" – just as he had anticipated. 6'6" wasn't a great mark, but it was good enough – especially under the conditions. Skinny Billy won the state championship!

His goal-setting, determined approach to both his academic and athletic accomplishments had raised his own personal bar and cleared it.

The University of Utah coach decided to give him a partial track scholarship to supplement his academic scholarship. Two major goals achieved! Skinny Billy's goal setting approach to challenges changed his life – *and mine*. The teacher had become the student.

It didn't end there. During his first year in college, he took second in the Skyline Conference Championship jumping 6'9".

After his first year, he told me, "If I want to be as good as I can and get into med' school, I have got to stay on track and concentrate all of my time on being an outstanding student. I will not have time for athletics."

He had decided to concentrate solely on becoming a doctor – not just a doctor but, as he had determined when he was still in high school, a heart surgeon.

Have you ever heard of Skinny Billy? You probably have.

Skinny Billy not only achieved his goal of becoming a heart surgeon, he became a nationally renowned heart surgeon. In 1982, he made national news by implanting the first artificial heart, the Jarvik Heart, into a human being.

Skinny Billy is Dr. William DeVries.

2

Wade Bell

The Anatomy of Greatness

The first step in getting ahead is to take the first step. The second step is to not fall behind. The real trick to success in sports and in life is to get ahead and stay ahead – of you, not someone else.
  ~ Anonymous

Be like a postage stamp – stick to one thing until you get there.
  ~ Josh Billings

Always take home the girl you brought to the dance.
  ~ Curt Hislop ("Dad")

Wade Bell, another outstanding student athlete at Ben Lomond High School, personified and epitomized the concept of striving for one's own personal best – and letting the competition take care of itself.

I saw Wade win the city junior high school half-mile championship in the spring even before I received the coaching job at Ben Lomond. I saw great potential in him because of the natural smoothness of his stride, but when I talked to him over the summer it was obvious that he was unaware of his true ability. He didn't train very much. He won the race I had watched entirely on innate ability.

11

I told him he would be an outstanding distance runner if he was willing to put in the work. If he wanted to be good, he would have to increase his mileage. Wade responded with cautious positivity, but expressed some uncertainty about what exactly that would entail. I told him that we would start by running two or three miles a day, then we'd take it from there.

"When do we start?"

"First thing in the morning,"

He gave me a quizzical look. "In the morning? Tomorrow? Well, I have to be at my Dad's bakery by 8:00."

"That's great. It won't take us long to run a couple of miles. I will pick you up at your house at 6:30."

"6:30? In the morning? Us?"

"Yes, 'us.' We'll do it together. It will be perfect. Not too hot."

I turned and walked away.

We started off running together. He liked that.

After about a week of this routine, I went to pick him up and he was still in bed. He had pointed out his bedroom window earlier in the week, so I went over and knocked on the glass.

A sleepy, irritated voice responded, "What!"

"Wade! It's Coach. Come on, let's run!"

A few minutes later Wade stumbled through the front door blinking in the early morning light. He was not overly thrilled with the prospect of running that early, but off we went anyway. Once we got going, though, he seemed to enjoy it.

We were up to about three miles a day when I went to his house and for the second time found Wade asleep.

This time when I tapped on the window, Wade, yelled back, "Go away!"

"What?"

"Go away!"

"Oversleeping won't make your dreams come true, Wade. You will never achieve your personal best – or much of anything – that way."

The family bakery was just across the parking lot from the house, so I said, "Do you want me to go over and tell your parents that you don't want to get up and keep your word?"

"Wait a minute," he grumbled, "I'm coming."

Soon his reluctance faded and he started to look forward to his early morning runs. He would usually be outside waiting for me when I arrived.

At the end of the summer we were running three to five miles a day, five mornings a week. Since I was running with him, I could watch him carefully to determine how far and how hard he should run.

By the beginning of his sophomore year, Wade had decided that he wanted to become an outstanding runner. The idea of focusing on accomplishing his personal best had taken root. It soon became part of his character. I knew I had a champion on my hands.

That year progressed well. He made huge improvement. His mile pace was soon faster than his half-mile pace had been when we started working together. He qualified for the state meet and took third place – as a sophomore!

Wade started his junior year cross country season in 1962. At that time cross country was not yet a sanctioned sport in the state of Utah. There were, in fact, only two or three races where high-school cross country athletes could compete against each other.

Generally unable to get onto golf courses to hold races, as they do today, these events were essentially road races. We were preparing for a race against Weber High School, then located in Ogden Utah. To provide athletes with the opportunity of running fast times, the Weber coach decided to construct a downhill course.

Wade was running well but the downhill course took its toll. About half way through the course, he began to limp. He finished the race – and won – but the next morning he was barely able to walk. He couldn't put any pressure on his right leg. His mother took Wade to the doctor, who determined that Wade had pulled some of the muscles away from his hip and would not be able to run again for quite some time. In fact, the doctor recommended that he quit running for good.

With tears in his eyes, Wade told me the news from the doctor, but added, "Coach, I am going to continue to work out. I am going to run. I can't achieve my personal best if I quit!"

"Wade, I can't let you run against your doctor's orders."

He looked at me, a little disgusted, "Well… we'll see."

I was worried about him, so the next day I stopped by his first period class, to see how he was doing. Wade wasn't there. I called his house and asked if he was there. His mother said he was at school. When I told her that he wasn't there, we were both worried. I was in the gym when school ended. I saw Wade on crutches making his way across the floor toward me.

"Where have you been?" I asked.

"I went to see the doctor – and he said it is okay for me to run."

"What?"

"Here's his note."

In classic, nearly illegible doctor-scrawl, the note said that he could run – after a month of physical therapy.

I looked closely at the note. "Wade, this isn't the signature of your family doctor."

"I know. I went to see a different doctor."

"How did you get in touch with this doctor?"

"Well, he was the fifth doctor I saw today."

"What? Are you telling me that you looked for a doctor who would tell you what you wanted to hear?"

"Yup," he responded with a smile. "Actually, Coach, I decided to go to different doctors until I found one who understood why this was so important to me and who would work with me and help me. Doesn't that make sense?" Without waiting for an answer, he added, "So, how do we do this?"

He had to go through five doctors before he could find one that thought it could be done. The doctor assigned him to a physical therapist who prescribed a series of repair and strengthening exercises. The prescription was to use varying degrees of weight on each type of lift.

At that time weight training was in its infancy, especially for track & field programs, so our high school had no weights of any kind.

So we improvised. We went to the hardware store and bought five all-purpose buckets (I don't think the manufacturer anticipated this purpose). We put the buckets on the scale that we used to weigh-in the wrestlers. We poured sand into each bucket increasing the weight five pounds at a time. Five pounds of sand in the first bucket, ten pounds in the next, fifteen pounds in the third, etc.

Our weight program consisted of five sand-filled buckets. They ranged, in five-pound increments, from five to twenty-five pounds. A few cinder blocks, and a few feet of new rope, rounded out our weight training equipment.

Wade would sit on a table and I'd strap one of the bucket handles to his ankle with an old dog collar. He was then able to do the exercises the physical therapist had recommended. It worked. Wade grew stronger over the course of the winter. We outgrew the buckets and blocks and soon had to buy bigger buckets to fill with more sand.

With all of this extra work, running was beginning to be very important to Wade. He decided to write down exact goals for his running career. The first goal was to win the state championship in the mile. The second goal was even more ambitious. He determined that he would break the state record.

At the time, the state record was 4:32. It had stood for over twenty years. Wade was not content to just break the record; his more specific goal was to run a sub 4:30 mile. That was not enough. He also committed to writing a goal to set the state record in the 880[2]. We hadn't even been training for that.

I guess he figured as long as there was lead in the pencil, he might as well keep writing. While he was writing these ever-more-specific goals he decided that a long-term goal was to be the first person from his home state of Utah to run under four minutes in the mile.

At that time, only eight runners had run a sub four-minute mile – in the world! So I said, "Well, that goal is a ways off." After a pause,

2   The half-mile was then commonly referred to as the "the 880" – meaning eight hundred and eighty yards.

I added, "It is possible, but there are a few things you must do to get there."

"I know, Coach," Wade responded, "Number one, I have to pick the right college, one where the coach has some experience and can push me even harder than you're pushing me now."

He continued, "I've got to go someplace where I can compete on a regular basis. If I get beat my first couple years of college that is fine; it will just force me to continue improving."

He prefaced his last goal by saying, "Coach, you might tell me that this next one can't be done." He took a breath and continued, "I am going to make the Olympic Team."

"Wow! Yes, that is quite a goal! No, I won't tell you it can't be done. I will only say you haven't done it – yet."

"Yea, but I can do it, I just need the right mentor and do the right things – right? You told me all along that I have more talent than anyone else. So, if God has given me that, I have to use it the right way."

We all know about the "thrill of victory." How about the greater "thrill of personal accomplishment"? When an athlete begins to love challenge and adversity, and is focused on his personal best you know you've got a champion. In athletics this is also called a "PR" – one's own personal record. Great athletes focus more on their own personal records than the achievements of others. Isn't that how we should measure victory and success in business and in life – achieving our own personal best?

Wade's hip healed. By the end of his junior year he was running well. He accomplished his goal of running under 4:30 in the mile at the state meet – but he did not win. He came in second by one tenth of a second in a photo finish. Both runners ran a sub 4:30 for the first time in Utah state history. Wade ran 4:28.7 and the young man who won ran 4:28.6. Wade had accomplished one of his goals, but not both.

Wade started his senior year, and it was once again time for cross country competition. The Little Brown Jug Cross Country Race served as the city-county high school championship. It was typically held in the evening before a night football game.

The course went down a canyon into a rodeo arena where the football game was to be played. They ran down one side of the football field, in sand, and up the other side to the fifty-yard line.

Wade was so excited that he became unaware of his own speed. He caught up with the pace car (a police car with flashing red lights) and followed close behind for nearly two miles. The police car pulled off to the side as Wade entered the stadium. He reached the end of the football field and began his final turn around the goal post before the second place runner even entered the stadium.

One hundred and fifty yards ahead of the second place runner, Wade suddenly slowed drastically and started to stagger. He could barely stand. Unable to maintain his lead, two runners passed him. As he crossed the finish line, he passed out.

Watching one of my athletes pass out – waiting to see whether or not he would be okay – that was one of the scariest situations of my coaching career. Later, the doctor said that not only was he suffering from exhaustion and dehydration from pushing the pace, but he had also been following the police car too closely and had gotten carbon monoxide poisoning from the exhaust. For two days, he was sick as a hound dog after eating road kill!

This experience did not deter Wade from pursuing his goals. He continued to run well. As a senior he set a state record in the mile at 4:24. Another goal bites the dust! He also won the half mile, becoming the first person to win both races in the state meet and achieving an "unset goal."

When one achieves much, one generally achieves much more than planned.

His achievements began to attract serious attention, and he began to be recruited heavily by coaches around the state. These were good, respectable programs, but Wade's goal was to be trained by someone who had proven his ability to coach a four minute miler.

This was 1964. There were not many in the United States who had coached a four minute miler. Bill Bowerman was one of a few who had. He was an exceptional coach at the University of Oregon.[3]

Wade decided he wanted to attend the University of Oregon. He chose the coach, not just the school.

He knew his 4:24 was good, but did not realize how good. Many high school runners ran faster times. But they were at sea level so most of us did not make the connection. Back then, no one knew how to convert altitude mile times to sea level times.

Our goal was to get Wade into the Golden West High School Invitational Track Meet held in Southern California. This would give him great experience with stiffer competition. This meet had only been running for four years, but was already considered the USA high school championship meet.

I called the race director. He told me that Wade's time was not fast enough to get him into the meet. I reminded him that his time was run at altitude. He still said "No." I sent him a picture of a mud-splattered Wade running in cold, wet conditions, through five inches of thick muddy water on a soggy cinder track at a Utah meet. You could see the fans in the background wrapped in blankets and huddled under umbrellas. This dramatic photograph impressed the race director. He decided to give Wade a chance.

The first thing we did when we arrived in Los Angeles for the meet was check out the heat sheets. We noticed that the slowest person

---

3   Bowerman made specialized shoes for some of his athletes. One of his inventions was the waffle sole – inspired by his wife's waffle iron. Bowerman was a cofounder of Nike

in the race, other than Wade, had a 4:16. At 4:24, Wade's time was twelve seconds slower than the top three runners.

The fastest three runners had times of 4:06, 4:08, and 4:10. At dinner that evening, one of those top three contenders sat down across from Wade. He spoke up sarcastically, "Who is this guy with the 4:24. What's he even doing in the race?

Wade looked steadily across the table and responded quietly, "I'm Wade Bell. My mile time is 4:24."

The table fell silent.

Had we bitten off more than we could chew?

With the strength of the field, we assumed that the race would start quickly, but no one wanted to take the lead. Like many national races, this turned into a tactical race. The first half-mile was a slow 2:13. Wade was certainly comfortable with that – especially given that this race was at sea level. The third lap quickened only slightly. The runners hit the three quarter mile mark at 3:18. Wade was right there with them.

At the gun-lap (now called the bell-lap) the pace changed dramatically. The runners took off. Wade stayed with them. As they went around the last turn, Wade stepped outside to make his move. Another runner (the one who had made the sarcastic remarks at the table) made his move at the same time. As he cut out, he nicked Wade's foot. From the stands I saw a shoe fly above everyone's head.

Wade ran the last 150 yards of the race, painfully, on a cinder track, with only one shoe.[4] He hit the straightaway at full bore. With 100 yards to go, three runners were running nearly abreast. Wade was slightly behind, but in a seemingly effortless move, he caught them, passed them, and won by a second – with one shoe!

---

4   Unlike today's rubber or synthetic surfaced track, tracks were surfaced with what they called "cinder" – abrasive crushed lava pressed into clay.

The overall time of 4:17 was not a terrific time, but the way he ran the race caught the heart of the crowd. A 58 second last lap and a 27 second final 220 yards proved his capability. There were some college coaches in the stands. Several asked me, "Where has he signed?"

"Well, he hasn't signed yet. He isn't sure where he is going."

When we got home the University of Utah, Utah State, and BYU all offered Wade scholarships.

But Wade was focused on what he wanted, on his own goals, not on what they were putting on the table.

"Coach, would you contact the University of Oregon for me and see if they are interested?"

I agreed to write a letter and, after about a week, Wade received a call from Coach Bowerman of the University of Oregon. He apologized for not knowing about Wade until the Golden West meet. Though he assumed that Wade had signed elsewhere, he wanted Wade to know that he was interested in him.

Wade flew to Eugene for a visit. Coach Bowerman offered him a partial scholarship and promised to help him find work to offset some of his college expenses. He got him a summer job at a local sawmill and a weekend job during the school year. Wade accepted Bowerman's offer.

This was difficult for Wade's parents. They were afraid that if their second oldest son went away to college, he might not come back to make his home in Utah where his family was. But they respected the program for its academics – and its reputation for having one of the best track & field programs in the country. They honored Wade's aspirations to improve as a runner and supported his decision to go to the University of Oregon.

Wade's sophomore year went well [at that time, freshmen could not compete on the varsity team]. Bowerman decided that Wade had greater potential in the half-mile than the mile.

That year when the big races came around, Wade ran the half-mile as a sophomore, placing in the National Collegiate Athletic Association (NCAA) meet achieving the status of All American. As a junior, Wade once again placed in the half mile again achieving the status of All American. He also continued to improve in the mile. He ran a 4:03.

Wade ran the half mile almost exclusively during his senior year, but had not lost sight of his goal to break the four minute mile. He had approached Coach Bowerman earlier that year to let him know that one of his goals in coming to the University of Oregon was to run a sub four-minute mile.

Bowerman agreed that Wade was ready so, toward the end of his senior year, they set up a race for him and one of his teammates to go under four-minutes in the mile.

I was unable to attend the race, but I saw the headline the following morning "U of O has two more run under 4:00." Wade had run 3:59.7 becoming the first native Utah runner to break the four-minute mile.

Another goal accomplished!

As luck would have it, that year, the NCAA Championships were to be held in Provo, Utah, at Brigham Young University. Wade was favored. Wade ran the 880 as he always did. After a calculated start, he surged dramatically from the back of the pack with about 300 yards to go. With 200 to go, he passed the field and extended his lead to about 15 yards. In front of 17,000 cheering Utahans, Wade won the 880 by one of the largest margins in NCAA history.

We were now one year away from the Olympic Games. Wade had graduated from college but he went back to the University of Oregon to continue training with his college coach.

The United States scheduled a meet in Los Angeles with the Russians and the United Kingdom [at that time, Kenya was still considered part of the UK]. With only six people in the race, Wade ran his signature race, beginning his surge with about 300 yards to go. He took the lead; then extended it to 10 yards with 100 yards to go.

This was a nationally televised meet. I was watching from Utah as one of the Kenyan runners made a bid to catch Wade. The Kenyan closed on him and passed him just after the finish line. Wade won by inches. The television crew came up to him after the race. He was still breathing hard, and one of the commentators said, "Good thing the race wasn't two yards longer or you wouldn't have won!"

Wade responded, "Well, I don't know what he was racing, but I was racing the 880 yard run, not the 882." Wade's time in that race, 1:45.00, was the second fastest 880-yard time in history. Once again he accomplished his goal.

After that outstanding race, Wade came back to Utah to rest before he went to Eugene to begin his final preparation for the Olympics. While he was in Utah, I asked him if he was going to make any changes in his race strategy. His answer was an emphatic, "No."

I said, "Won't everyone know how you are going to race?"

He replied, "Yes, but they won't know how I train for it and they won't train the way I do. This gives me the advantage. I'm gonna' stay on track. This strategy got me here. I'm not changing now."

The next year started off well for Wade. The Olympics were to be held in Mexico City. Because this was to be held at altitude (seven thousand feet above sea level) the United States Olympic Committee staged an early qualifying event at Lake Tahoe California (6800 foot altitude). They built a track especially to select the three participants that would likely represent the United States on the Olympic Team. There was to be a later meet held just a few weeks before the Olympic

Games in Los Angeles to demonstrate that these runners were still fit and ready to represent the United States in the Olympics.

Using the same tactics he had worked on for the past three years, Wade won at Lake Tahoe by more than ten meters. That qualified him for the Olympic Team. He again proved his fitness by winning in Los Angeles. This made him one of the favorites for an Olympic gold medal in Mexico City.

I read reports that three days before the Olympics, Wade had had a terrific workout. Bowerman felt that Wade would not only win, but that he could also make a bid for the world record.

After that fabulous workout, however, "Montezuma's Revenge" hit Wade. Terribly ill, he was unable to complete his Olympic Trials. The runner Wade had beaten in both Olympic Trial races took the bronze. Wade was crushed. He knew where he could have finished.

After the Olympics, Wade came home to Utah. For the first two weeks he was back, he spent at least sixteen hours a day at my home to avoid people asking questions about his experience. This was a very difficult time in his life. He had met all of his other goals, but his experience at the Olympics left him feeling like a failure.

Originally, he had only hoped to make the Olympic Team. Once he made the team, however, he set his sights higher. He determined to be an Olympic Champion. He planned his race, and raced his plan – yet felt as though he had failed.

Wade finally came to understand that he had given one hundred percent, but the circumstances were simply out of his control. Stuff happens. It is true on the track. It is true in life.

Wade moved forward and created a very successful life using the success principles that made him a great runner. He established tangible goals in life and in business and implemented strategies for their accomplishment. He accomplished his goals in life with the same focus and determination he had in his bid for his Olympic dream. He created a great life for himself, his family and those who look to him for leadership.

That is success.

3

Todd Parker

A Winning Trajectory

It's not the will to win that matters – everyone has that. It's the will to prepare to win that matters.
  ~ Coach Paul "Bear" Bryant

Focus on solutions, not problems.
  ~ Anonymous

Remember that triumph is just a little "umph" added to "try."
  ~ Author Unknown

I first met Todd Parker when he was in the ninth grade. He was competing in the City County Junior High School Track & Field Championships. He was one of three pole-vaulters from Mound Fort Jr. High School in Ogden. He didn't break a record or do anything else particularly notable. I don't even remember if he won that day. What struck me was how small he was in comparison to the other vaulters. He was perhaps 5'2" or 5'3" and shy of 100 pounds, but he was vaulting the same as everyone else.

He started at Ben Lomond High School in the fall at the same time I held my annual meeting for those interested in running cross country. I always encouraged athletes who were interested in track & field to run cross country, if they were not playing football, because it would give me a chance to find out what they were made of.

Todd was too small to play football, so I tracked him down and asked him if he would go out for cross country. He asked me if it would help him in the pole vault.

I said, "Sure! Cross country will help you be a better pole vaulter."

What did I know? I was as enthused about him as I was uninformed about the pole vault. What I really wanted to do was be his coach. Why? Because I knew he was willing to work.

I had only been a coach for two or three years. Not only did I know next to nothing about pole vaulting, my ignorance was deepened by the fact that it was also a transitional era for the event. Flexible fiberglass poles were replacing the traditional steel poles. The technique was different with the new poles, and I certainly did not know how to coach it. I told Todd that if he would come out for cross country I would learn everything I possibly could about pole vaulting so I could coach him there as well.

It was a deal. Todd came out for cross country and, as I suspected, worked hard – very hard. By the end of the season he was running as our seventh or eighth man and was close to making the varsity team. As the winter progressed, Todd came to me and said, "Coach, I want to start working on the pole vault – right now."

I had done my homework. I had researched the technique differences between vaulters using fiberglass poles those using the traditional steel pole. I realized that the technique differences were significant.

One difference was hand placement. With the rigid steel pole, vaulters would slide their hands together as they planted the pole in the box. With the fiberglass pole, proper hand positioning required that the hands be placed about eighteen inches apart on the run-up and *stay* that far apart when the pole was planted in the box. This enabled the vaulter to pull down on the top hand and push up on the bottom hand, facilitating the initial bend in the flexible pole. In order to keep the hands separate the vaulter needed a lot of strength in his forearms and shoulders.

One of the articles I read during my research said that a vaulter ought to be able to climb a rope using only his arms without wrapping his legs around the rope for support. I told Todd that one of the first things he had to be able to do was climb a rope forty feet – to the top of the gym, hand-over-hand, employing only the strength of his arms. On his first try, he managed to get to the top but he had to use his legs. He could only go hand over hand a couple of times before he had to use his legs to keep from sliding down the rope.

His first objective, then, was to master the rope climb. One day, after about a month of working on the rope climb, he came to me with a triumphant grin, "Coach, I can do it! I can climb to the top without using my legs."

"How many times have you done it?"

"Once."

I casually replied, "Oh, you have to be able to do it at least five times," and I went off to wrestling practice.

During that winter, he worked on his rope climbing, while I researched fiberglass poles. Our school did not have one. I discovered that the poles were sold by sizes based on body weight. The smallest pole available was for a person who weighed 120 pounds. [This was long before women started pole-vaulting.] Even though he was a sophomore, Todd weighed less than one hundred pounds.

The school purchased the lowest weight-rated pole available and Todd worked his entire sophomore year on a fiberglass pole that he was unable to bend. Nevertheless, there was enough give that he was able to work on and improve his technique.

I was constantly amazed at how hard he worked. Everyday Todd was the first one on the practice field and the last one to leave.

Because athletes vault higher with the fiberglass pole, they need a softer place to land. At that time our landing pit consisted of sawdust surrounded by hay bales. At the end of his sophomore year, Todd approached me, "Coach, there are schools that have foam rubber pits. Is there any way we could get one?"

I went to the high school administrator who informed me that the school could not afford such a pit. We had to innovate. That's okay. We were used to doing that. We would create our own foam rubber pit. I went to an old junk car lot, explained the situation to the owner, and asked if we could cut the foam out of old car seats. He agreed. Todd and I, with the help of four of his friends, spent several Saturdays filling the bed of my pickup with old foam cut from car seats.

Copying the design of the expensive foam mats, we made our own bags. My wife, Dianne, helped us cut out the patterns and pieces. She tried to sew them but our machine wasn't tough enough. We enlisted the help of someone with an industrial sewing machine.

We started with a canvas lining for the bottom and about eight inches up the sides. We filled each of these bags with our car-seat foam, tied a mesh cover over the top of the foam and fastened it to the canvas bottom to complete the bag. That worked for a minute or two, but the foam tended to shift and after four or five jumps, the vaulters would hit the ground.

Maybe we didn't have enough foam in the bags. We opened them up again and stuffed in as much foam as we possibly could, pulled the mesh back over the foam and fastened it down tightly. That looked better. But the bags were now too full and firm. The vaulters would hit and the trampoline effect would bounce the vaulter right out of the pit.

After a great deal of experimentation with bag size, tension, fullness, etc., we achieved an appropriate balance of give and firmness.

By now we were well into the fall of Todd's junior year. Our innovative home-made landing pad now consisted of three large bags four feet wide by eight feet long placed side by side which made our pole vault pit twelve feet wide by eight feet deep. This worked okay – but it wasn't perfect. It was a definite improvement from the old sawdust and hay bale pit – but it did not provide room for error.

By this time in my career, I was co-coaching our high school's wrestling program. After seeing how hard Todd worked during his sophomore year and what a focused, hard worker he was in general, I asked him if he would come out for the wrestling team. Until then, Todd had done everything that I had asked of him and had never turned me down. But that day he turned me down flat.

Without hesitation he said, "No, Coach, I can't do that."

"But it will help build your strength and help you be a better pole vaulter."

"No! I can't do that!"

Later that year I found out why he had so adamantly refused. He knew I would want him to wrestle at the 98-pound weight class. He had finally broken the 100-pound mark. He now weighed 102. He didn't want to do anything that would make him smaller or take any of his hard-built strength away. His goal was to get to 105 that winter and he thought that the weight control that is required in wrestling would jeopardize his strength-building for pole vaulting.

He continued to work on rope climbing and the other exercises I asked of him; push-ups, pull-ups, and sit-ups. At that time, pole vaulters did not use the weight room; therefore, all of his strength training involved lifting his body weight.

During the winter of his junior year, he came up to the wrestling room and said, "Coach, when you get a minute, come to the gym. I wanna show you something."

I finished practice and went down to see him. He rosined his hands and climbed the rope without touching it with his legs. He came down, applied some more rosin and did it again. With no more than fifteen seconds between climbs, Todd climbed that rope five consecutive times. When he finished he looked at me and said, "Now what?"

As I continued my research into the use of fiberglass poles in vaulting, I discovered that there were different positions the vaulter needed to be in before pushing off the pole to clear the bar. One involved the vaulter inverting his posture, almost becoming a human ball with his hips and rump above his head and his knees tucked down close to the shoulders. This is referred to as "the rock-back position."

I knew Todd was familiar with this, so in answer to his question as to what to work on next, I said, "You are about half-way there. You've done the *easy* half. Now I want to see you climb the rope in the rock-back position. That means with your hips above your shoulders and your knees tucked into your shoulders. Can you climb that rope upside down?"

He looked at me strangely and asked, "How many times?"

"Well, let's just get one before we worry about that."

"But you are *going* to tell me *five times*, aren't you?" Todd pressed.

"Yeah. Eventually. But we won't worry about that for a while."

I turned on my heel and headed for the wrestling room, leaving him muttering, "What do you mean 'we'?"

This is what Todd worked on the winter of his junior year – along with all the other things I asked him to do. By the end of his sophomore year, he had vaulted twelve feet. He was also managing to get just a bit of a bend out of the fiberglass pole – not nearly enough of a bend to do any good, but he was making progress.

By the end of his junior year Todd had vaulted 12'9".

We had made a deal at the beginning of his junior year. Todd would have to clear thirteen feet before he was a senior or he would give up the pole vault and concentrate on cross country and wrestling.

We were signing yearbooks on the last day of school Todd's junior year. He walked up to me and said, "Coach, I've got to do more. I've got to practice all summer so I can learn to bend the pole more so that I can win the state championship and set the state record."

"Wait a minute, Todd. Why are you talking about winning a championship when you aren't even going to vault next year?"

"I have three months between now and when my senior year begins. I still get to try."

What could I say? I might have been able to argue the point, but my job is to encourage excellence. "Well, okay. We will do whatever we possibly can."

He planned on working at the college that summer from 1PM to 7PM, but his mornings were free. He wanted to practice then. I was working a graveyard shift during the summer to make ends meet, so I agreed to meet him at the high school at 8AM to drag the pit out for practice.

Our track was about three hundred yards away from the gym where we stored our makeshift landing mats. The mats had accumulated some water over the preceding year making them very heavy.

We couldn't drag them very far, so once again we improvised. We decided to use the parking lot adjacent to the gym as our practice arena.

We made a pole vault box and a runway right down the middle of the parking lot. (Sometimes it's better to ask forgiveness than permission.) There were times I couldn't stay to the end of the workout, so he had to either pull those mats back into the gym himself or recruit friends to help him.

Three days a week, all summer long, Todd practiced pole-vaulting in the mornings before he went to his job at the college. He talked openly with his friends and new acquaintances about his aspirations in the pole vault. He became acquainted with a Weber State basketball player by the name of Monte Vrenon. Monte also happened to be a vaulter. He had, in fact, won the pole vault championship in the Big Sky Conference that year.

Todd asked him to check out what he was doing and see if he had any suggestions.

Monte's personal coaching helped immensely but, for the most part, Todd practiced alone that summer. Other than my occasionally being there, no one was there to help him drag out the mat, set and reset the bar, or catch his pole. It was evidence of his dedication and personal focus.

He could now bend the pole a little more. During practice, he cleared 13'6." Though still shy of the state record mark, it was a great achievement. It earned his right to continue to vault his senior year and it put him in position to win.

That winter, Todd continued to work on his upper body strength primarily through his rope climbing practice. He came to my classroom one day and asked me to meet him before practice – he had something else to show me.

We met in the gym. Todd stretched out and warmed up, applied some rosin to his hands, grabbed the rope, flipped over into the rock-back, upside-down position with his knees above his head and proceeded to climb to the top of the rope – upside down!

He reached the ceiling, then came down, rested for about thirty seconds, applied more rosin to his hands and went right back up again. He repeated the process five times in rapid succession.

Todd became the talk of the school. He was known as the guy who could climb the rope upside-down. I had promised him that if he could do this, he could accomplish his goal of winning the state championship and breaking the state record.

I had a couple of concerns, though. One was that we needed a bigger pit. Our homemade pit was too small and too dangerous to vault at the heights that Todd was achieving. After much thought, I wrote a letter addressed to the principal of the high school and the district superintendent. I noted the rule from the National High School Federation Rule Book which stated the size of a pole vault landing pit should be 12' x 15' and that ours was short at 8' x 12'. I told them it was a safety issue and that I was putting this in writing so I would not be held responsible if something happened to Todd. The principal read the letter and said he would show it to the superintendent that day.

When I got to school the next day there was a note on my door from the principal telling me to come to his office. Attached was a price list showing the cost of a new pit.

Todd had a safe pit within two weeks!

My other concern was that I might not be qualified to coach him at the level necessary to take him where he needed to go. I felt I had to get him more help and a better mentor. I recognized my lack of expertise in this particular area and didn't think I could teach him the technique that would get him in position to win the state championship. I needed someone to help me coach him – or take over the job altogether.

The basketball coach at Weber State College told me that Monte Vrenon, the same young man Todd had met the summer between his junior and senior year, was going to do his student teaching during the upcoming spring quarter. I made arrangements with the education department at the college to have Monte do his student teaching at our high school so he could coach Todd.

Unfortunately, the college track coach would not let Monte vault at the high school. Monte did his student teaching at the high school, practice his vaulting at the college, then return to the high school to coach Todd. Todd would study from the time the high school let out until around 5:00 in the evening; waiting for Monte to finish his own practice at the college and return to the high school.

As cumbersome as this process was, those practice sessions became a great learning experience – for me. It was wonderful to watch Monte help Todd develop his technique.

Again, the teacher learns from the student.

Monte helped Todd throughout his senior year, and by the time of the state meet Todd was jumping 14' – an inch away from the 14'1" state record.

Todd entered the state meet as the favorite. He was ready for the championship. He was now 5'6" and almost 120 pounds, but he was still the smallest pole vault competitor at the meet. As he warmed up, I heard someone say, "Oh, look at the cute little sophomore."

As Todd began his warmup vaults, however, it became clear that he was better than the other vaulters. We had to be careful not to start Todd at too low of an opening height to avoid knocking the pole off on the way down. They started the vaulting at about 10'6". We waited.

When the bar reached 12' there were only five other people left in the competition. A typical rule-of thumb in vaulting is to start about a foot and a half below where the jumper should vault that day. That meant Todd should wait until the bar reached about 12'8."

By that time, there were only three other vaulters left. The two and-a-half-hour wait had made Todd nervous. His first jump was a miserable attempt. He did not keep his arms straight. He let his body get in too close to the pole. He did not even get close to the crossbar.

Two of the other competitors also made their first attempt at this height. Now, in order for Todd to win, he needed to not only clear this height but clear a higher height as well. We knew he was capable, but I was concerned. On his second attempt, Todd came much closer to making his attempt, but he came too close and clipped the bar on the way up, knocking it from the stand.

After three years of hard work, and all of the effort that Todd had put into training for, and reaching, his goal in the pole vault, he was in serious risk of ending up a "no height." One more attempt at 12'8" would determine whether or not he would even place in the state meet. The memory of what happened next is etched indelibly on my mind.

Todd walked slowly to the starting point on the runway for his third and final attempt at 12'8". He turned – and just stood there. With his pole resting on his shoulder, he stared at the cross bar one hundred and twenty feet away. He stood quietly.

Back then, there was no time limit. Todd waited – and waited. What was going on? Was he scared? What was he doing? What was he thinking? Two or three minutes of Todd waiting to jump felt like an hour. Finally Todd bowed his head – and I knew exactly what he was doing. Todd was a spiritual young man. I knew the depth of his faith. As he bowed his head, that faith was what he was tapping into.

He raised his head, smiling confidently. He charged down the runway. He positioned his arms perfectly for the takeoff, made a perfect plant and tucked back into the rock-back position. His push off from the pole was so powerful and perfect that he soared over the crossbar, clearing it by nearly two feet. I was worried he might knock the bar off on his way down. He didn't. It was a beautiful, perfectly timed jump.

He walked casually back from the pit. Instead of appearing jubilant, he acted as if this was just part of the experience – just part of his job – for a man of faith, it likely was.

Now, the bar was only being raised in 3" increments. The next height was 12'11". The first vaulter missed. The second made it. Now it was Todd's turn. Again, he just sat there on a bench at the side of the runway.

I called out, "Todd, what are you doing?"

"I am passing Coach. I know I can make it; and I want to save my attempts."

Our plan before the meet started was to vault, then pass a height, then vault. Despite having struggled on his first height, Todd was sticking to the plan. I was certainly willing to deviate a bit from the original plan, given what had just happened, but Todd wasn't. He passed, and the bar was raised.

After passing at 13'1", Todd cleared on his first attempt at 13'4". One of the other vaulters cleared it as well. The third didn't clear and was out of the competition. It is down to two competitors. The other knew he had Todd beaten on misses. The officials were conferring with the vaulters to determine the next height for the bar.

As the officials were measuring the new height, I called out to Todd, "What are they doing?"

"They are checking to make sure the bar is set high enough to break the state record," he called back.

"You are passing to a state record?" I asked incredulously.

He said, "The other vaulter wants to, so it's fine with me."

The other vaulter had nothing to lose because he had Todd beaten on misses. In order to beat *him*, though, Todd would have to clear a record-setting height.

Todd walked to the end of the runway and, without hesitation, turned, ran down the runway and again executed a near-perfect vault.

He sailed over the bar, setting a new state record.

Goal number one achieved.

The other young man missed; he didn't come close to the height. Todd won the state championship.

Goal number two achieved.

But...

Instead of calling it quits, he asked the officials to raise the bar. Todd cleared the new height, setting another state record.

By now, the entire stadium had turned their attention away from the rest of the track meet to the pole vault.

That wasn't good enough for him. Todd asked for the bar to be raised again.

Again he cleared the bar, setting his *third* state record of the day. He did something that had never been done – he set a new state record three times in a matter of minutes. When he cleared the bar, the excitement – the roar from the crowd was unbelievable.

"Good enough" was simply not "good enough" for Todd. This undersized young man who was once classified as a "98-pound weakling," had trained his body and mind to do something at which most people would marvel.

He walked out of the pit – with a little more enthusiasm this time – and waved at the crowd. Inside, he was bursting with excitement and well-earned pride at his accomplishment.

I asked Todd after the competition why he had taken so much time before his third attempt at 12'8".

He said, "Coach, I was reviewing every step of the runway and the plant in my mind. I wanted to make certain that I was doing everything just right. I reviewed in my mind each detail of my approach, my plant, take-off, rock-back position, push-off, and my flyaway. I wasn't going to make my last attempt before I had everything perfectly planned, rehearsed and visualized. Once I was certain I was on track, I paused to thank the Lord for the privilege of being able to pole vault, for being there that day, and for allowing me to do the best I was capable of.

Then I did it."

4

David Broderick

The S.P.A.M. Theorem

Obstacles don't have to stop you. If you run into a wall,
don't turn around and give up. Figure out how to climb it, go
through it, or work around it.
  ~ *Michael Jordan*

Excellence is never an accident
  ~ *Aristotle*

There are no traffic jams on the road to success; but there are
toll booths – the journey ain't free.
  ~ *Coach Chick Hislop*

Do or do not. There is no try.
  ~*Yoda*

Have you ever wondered why some athletes seem to love working
out while others feel it is drudgery? After coaching for about fifteen
years, I decided to find out why that was.

One afternoon, during a team meeting, I handed each of my athletes a
pen and paper and asked them to answer the following two questions:

Do you like to work out?
Why or why not?

Their answers were enlightening.

There were about thirty athletes on the team that year. I assumed their responses would fall into a twenty/ten ratio. Twenty would like it. Ten would not.

To my surprise the result was twenty-seven to three. Only nine percent viewed working out as drudgery. They did not enjoy it. It was no fun. They felt obligated. They had a different perception of what "working out" was. They saw no value in their efforts. Those three were also the bottom three – the under-achievers on the team.

The ninety-one percent, who enjoyed working out, enjoyed hard work. They also had a different perception of what working out meant. They perceived it as a means of improving and achieving – of scoring in the conference meet or becoming an All-American. They saw hard work as a means to an end, focused on the end result, and that is why they enjoyed the means. Working out was still work. It was their position, their attitude that made the difference.

I asked myself, "Why was it that some people feel this way, while others do not?

I found my answer in the grocery store. One day I was walking down the aisle, looking for my favorite breakfast food (Wheaties, of course; the "Breakfast of Champions"). My eye caught something on the shelf that shouted out the answer. It was a can of SPAM.

"SPAM?" I thought for a minute and said, "Yep, that's the answer." I purchased a can and brought it home and handed it to my wife, excitedly proclaiming, "This is it! This is the answer!"

She looked at it, then at me as if I had finally lost what was left of my mind. "SPAM? That's the answer to what? Indigestion?"

"No! It's the *real* breakfast of champions. It's the answer to success in life! It's the answer to everything! Look at the bottom of the can

– there's a key right there! See it? There it is the key to everything. SPAM makes people enjoy life – all of it – and succeed at everything. Yep, SPAM! S – P – A – M."

Super, Positive, Attitude, Mentally! SPAM is the key to a happy life. The key to excelling in athletics, life, marriage… Yes. Have a Super Positive Attitude Mentally.

My best athletes proved my SPAM theorem. One in particular exemplified this more than any other. He embodied the concept.

David Broderick had a Super Positive Attitude Mentally in every situation. People loved Dave. He would go into a restaurant and talk to anyone and everyone – and they would talk to him. By the time he left, everyone knew Dave and Dave knew everyone – by name. He made a point to learn his server's name and something about him or her.

His team called him "Governor" because of his positive, outgoing personality and the fact that he would talk to everyone and remember their names. I don't think he was ever served a meal by someone whom he did not know by the time the meal was over.

When I asked him about this, he explained, "Each time I enter a room, I find more friends." He was right! Everyone who *knows* Dave *likes* Dave.

One day, about two thirds of the way through Dave's freshman year, he came to my office with a worried look on his face. "Coach, I am having a hard time making ends meet. I have to come up with a way to get through school and still pole vault."

"Well, you are not on much of a scholarship, so if you have to maybe you could get a part-time job."

"Yeah, Coach, but I hate do that because it will interfere with my studies, working out, and my social life. I want to come up with a better way."

43

A month later, he came to my office again and said, "Coach, guess what I've done?"

"Dave, what have you done now?"

"I bought a house!"

"You bought a house?"

"Yep! I bought a house."

"And why did you buy a house, Dave?"

"So I won't have to work."

"How do you figure that?"

"Well, I bought a six bedroom house."

"A six-bedroom house? And that's not gonna' be work?"

"Yeah, two of the bedrooms are pretty big, and I can put two beds in those. I will live in one of the nicer rooms, and rent the remainder of the house to seven other guys."

"You are going to rent your house to seven people?" I asked evenly.

"Yep. I'll rent my house to seven guys for $150 to $200 per month each. After covering my mortgage, I figure I'll come out ahead about $500 per month or so – plus I won't be paying rent."

And that is how Dave financed his next four years of college.

He kept the house for a couple more years after he graduated; then sold it for a nice profit. Dave thrived with a steady diet of SPAM. With his Super Positive Attitude Mentally, he was constantly looking for, and finding, ways to improve himself, his circumstances, his life – and the lives of those around him.

Dave practiced all summer between his sophomore and junior year to improve his vaulting. One afternoon he was in such a hurry to get in a workout that he accidentally set the standards up backwards. There was a bolt protruding on the inside from one of the standards. On one of his jumps, he didn't quite make it into the pit. On his way down, his leg hit this bolt and tore a deep gash in his leg muscle.

He drove himself to the hospital where it took twenty stitches to piece together and hold his muscle together, and sixty-seven stitches to close up the external wound.

When he was finally off his crutches, he had a noticeable limp. He worked hard trying to strengthen his leg to get back into the routine of serious training, but his leg simply would never adequately recover. It was time to quit, but SPAM wouldn't let him. There had to be a way. There was a way, it just wasn't obvious.

Instead of competing the next year, he red-shirted – and attempted to vault in practice. His injured leg was his takeoff leg. Though not without an obvious limp, he was able to run fairly well; but he had no lift in this leg, consequently his pole vaulting was seriously compromised. Dave was a plus-15' vaulter before his injury, but he could not even clear 13' a year after the accident.

Dave somehow knew he would figure out a way to get back to vaulting. It was at the end of his red-shirt year that he came up to my office with excitement in his eyes – and a plan.

"Coach, I know what I can do! I figured out a way that I can vault again."

"What's that Dave?"

"I am going to vault left-handed."

"You are going to *what* left-handed?"

"Vault. As long as I don't have to use my bad leg as my take off leg, I can do it!"

I mustered the best, most conciliatory tone possible. "Dave, do you know how hard it would be to re-train yourself to vault left-handed?" I didn't want to be pessimistic, but I did want to present him with a sense of reality. I failed to realize that "reality" is not something that athletes with a diet of SPAM recognize very easily.

"Yeah, I know. I tried it a little yesterday. It's gonna' be tough."

"Dave, it's like learning how to pitch left-handed. At your age..." I trailed off.

"Maybe, maybe... But I can do it! I can!"

One of the first things he did in his quest to develop a left-handed vault was a lesson in re-programming. Again the teacher learns from the student. He found a broken pole, cut it off to about four feet long, and carried it around with him wherever he went. Every fifteen steps he would take the pole with his left hand on top instead of his right and raise it up over his head as if he were vaulting from the left side of his body.

Fellow students around campus looked at him as though he were a bit strange – walking to class with his backpack and his short pole vault pole that he would shoot up over his head every so many steps.

He progressed until he could plant left-handed and get up in the air pretty well. His challenge now was to learn to twist in the opposite direction over the crossbar – opposite of the direction his body was trained to turn – without knocking the crossbar off the standards.

His red-shirt year was up and he returned to the team. He continued to work hard, but he still wasn't good enough to make the traveling squad. He had to vault at least 14'6" and while he had cleared 13" he was nowhere near the 15'6" that he had been before his accident.

He was not able to make the traveling squad throughout his junior year; but his steady diet of SPAM gave him the energy, focus, and determination to continue to improve.

When he reached his senior year, he was fairly efficient at his left-handed vault. He had become a favorite among the team because they knew what he was doing – how impossible *it* was yet how positive *he* was. Whenever he was asked why he was even trying this, his response was always, "I can do it. I will do it. Besides, it's fun! "

During his senior year, he was vaulting consistently at 15'. He was finally traveling with the team.

He now weighed about one hundred fifty pounds, but was using a pole rated for a one hundred forty pound vaulter. The pole was bending too much; "too soft" we called it. He wanted to get on a higher rated pole necessary for an increased height at his weight. We got one for him but, because of his compromised left leg, he could not muster the speed of approach necessary to create the impact required to bend the higher rated pole.

At the conference meet, I was hoping he might be able to score some points for us by placing sixth or seventh. He brought both poles, but I didn't think he'd have any chance to use his bigger pole. I knew he could score some points for the team with the softer pole, but it would likely limit his personal best.

The day of the meet he said, "Coach, today is the last day I will ever vault – in my life. I am going to try the bigger pole."

"Okay Dave, but before you try the bigger pole be sure you place on your smaller pole so that we can gain points for the team."

They started the warm-up for the pole vault. I was down on the infield when I heard a loud "pop." I turned just in time to see Dave tumble head-first into the pit. The smaller pole had shattered, sending pieces of fiberglass flying in all directions. (Later, a woman who had been sitting about fifteen rows up in the stands brought me a piece of that broken pole.)

I thought, "Oh no, after all his hard work he won't be able to vault." Two minutes later, Dave came up to me full of enthusiasm. "Coach! Did you see that? Breaking my pole is the best thing that could have happened! Now I *have* to get on that big pole! This will be the best day of my life!"

He was excited. I was worried. He had never been able to make the bigger pole bend enough to even get him to the crossbar – and now he was enthusiastic about being forced to use it?

Talk about SPAM!

And he did it! He cleared 15 feet; then 15'4" – a new *left-handed* personal record for him.

Then he made 15'8". That set a second personal left-handed record. Then he cleared 15'10", a personal record with *either* hand. This became his third consecutive personal best of the afternoon.

Dave barely missed 16 feet, finishing second place at the conference meet – the highest he had placed in any meet in three years! He had gone into the meet tied for eighth in the rankings and came out an All-Conference performer in his last conference meet.

That's the kind of achievement a Super Positive Attitude Mentally will get you!

Is there a world record for a duel-handed vaulter? Well, yes, there is now. Adding the heights of his right and left-handed vaults, Dave's mark is 31'4"!

After Dave graduated from college, he sold his six-bedroom house, and went into business. By the time he was thirty-five years old, he had made his first million.

His success is largely because everything that happens to him, he transforms into a positive experience. He always looks at the bright side of life with a deeply held belief that life is *supposed* to be difficult. That's how we find ways to stay on track and continually improve no matter the challenge or opposition.

Dave lives on a steady diet of SPAM!

5

Vance Anderson

The Wheels of Misfortune

What really matters is what happens in us, not to us.
   ~ *James W. Kennedy*

It isn't the size of the dog in the fight; it's the size of the fight in the dog.
   ~ *Mark Twain*

It's not whether you get knocked down; it's whether you get up.
   ~*Vince Lombardi*

A champion is someone who gets up when he can't.
   ~ *Jack Dempsey*

It ain't over till it's over.
   ~ *Yogi Berra*

People always noticed Vance because he was small, yet well developed. He was already shaving by the time he was a sophomore in high school. He was about 5'1" or 5'2" and weighed 110 – 115 pounds when I met him. Throughout his high school career, his weight never got above 115. Naturally, I thought "wrestler."

Yes, Vance did wrestle for the high school, and he did well, but the nature of the sport was a struggle for him. Vance was very much an introvert. Walking out onto the mat in wrestling tights was embarrassing. He avoided warming up with his teammates and, only just before his match, would he take off his sweatpants. He'd go onto the mat, wrestle, and then put his sweats on immediately after. He was developing into an outstanding wrestler, but by the spring of his sophomore year it became apparent that wrestling was not his first love.

Vance Anderson wanted to be a discus thrower.

He was just asking for failure. How could a little 115 pounder throw the discus well enough to qualify for a region meet or any type of competition? He would have to face off against 200-250 pound throwers who were often over six feet tall.

Size seemed to make no difference to Vance. He wanted to be a discus thrower and that's just what he was going to be. At the end of his sophomore year, he asked me if he could take home a couple discuses for the summer.

Curiously, I asked, "Where will you throw them?"

Vance had planned it all out. "We have some fruit trees in my back yard. I can throw the discus from off the patio. They will hit the fruit trees – so they won't go into the neighbor's yard."

I didn't say much. I just sent the discuses home with him. He practiced all summer. When he came back, he had made a startling improvement. He could now throw about 115 feet which, in distance, was the equivalent of his body weight. This equivalent of a foot-distance-per-pound of body weight was a rough measure of what an *outstanding* thrower could do. The state record was about 170 feet and most of the best throwers in the state were at least two hundred pounds. If one of the other bigger throwers was able to get even close to his body weight, he could set a state record.

Before competition started his junior year, Vance was able to throw 125 feet. This was unheard of. At just 115 pounds he was throwing ten feet above his body weight. While this mark was not good enough to place in meets, it was amazing progress.

Summer came between his junior and senior years. Vance asked for the discuses again. This time he said, "Coach, I will ride my bicycle to the high school and practice the discus there."

"That's a couple miles. Why would you want to do that?"

"Oh, well... Mom thinks it would just be better if I came up here to practice."

I shrugged my "okay."

I later found out that over the previous summer, Vance had thrown the discus so much that, to his mother's dismay, he had broken so many limbs off the fruit trees that they wouldn't bear fruit the next season.

My house wasn't too far from the high school, so I would stop by the high school every afternoon to check on Vance. I always found his bike leaning against the fence. Little Vance would be out on the field throwing the discuses. He would throw two discuses, jog out to get them, and repeat the process – again and again and again.

One Saturday afternoon I took my kids to a matinee movie. As we passed the high school on the way to the movie we saw Vance practicing. We enjoyed the movie and had lunch. On the way back (three hours later), Vance was still out there throwing the discuses and running out to retrieve them.

He worked hard all that summer between his junior and senior years. Early in the fall of his senior year, he asked me to come out and measure his throws. Vance was throwing between 130 to 140 feet.

This was considered a fairly competitive mark among high school athletes. For Vance, it was an amazing personal accomplishment.

I asked him, "Do you think you are throwing better?"

"Yeah. I am throwing better, Coach," he replied casually.

What I witnessed was truly amazing. It wasn't just an issue of distance, his speed and precision was unbelievable. To this day, I have yet to witness anyone at any level of competition with greater skill, speed and technique in the discus ring than that high school kid demonstrated that day.

He had two throws over 150 feet. That was far enough to place in the state meet. He was throwing 35 feet further than his body weight. That little 115 pounder became a giant of a man when he stepped into the discus ring. Pound for pound, he was the best thrower *in the world*. If there was an archive of discus throws based on the thrower's body weight Vance would hold the all-time world record.

I had watched Glenn Passey win at the NCAA Championships. He weighed 187 pounds and won the championship with a throw of just over 190 feet. The world record holder, at the time, LJ Sylvester, was on the team with me at Utah State, but neither LJ nor Glenn could match the speed, precision, or technique of Vance Anderson.

During the winter of his senior year, Vance worked hard in the weight room to improve his strength. On President's Day, I was out on the field working with some of the other track athletes. It was a school holiday and there were several young children playing in and around the high school. Vance was in the weight room doing squats. He had completed a squat with three hundred pounds on the bar and, just as he was preparing to drop the weight to the floor, a little girl ran close by him. To protect the child, Vance made a quick move and caught the weight in mid-drop. In the process he twisted his back, crushing his eleventh and twelfth vertebrae, and fell limp to the floor.

The pressure of the immense weight (nearly three times his body weight) combined with his twisting motion, crushed two vertebrae, instantly paralyzing him from his waist down.

From that day forward Vance would be a paraplegic, unable to live the rest of his life in a manner that most would consider "normal." But "normal" had never been a goal for Vance. Before he left the hospital he told me he wanted to walk across the stage to receive his diploma like everyone else.

He was determined not to be in a wheelchair. Instead, he was determined to learn to walk with the aid of crutches. He knew it would take the same focus, technique, determination and practice that created his success as a discus thrower.

And he did it. He would balance on crutches, drag his feet under him, balance on his braced legs, move the crutches forward, shift his balance to the crutches, and drag his feet forward again. This is how Vance determined that he was going to learn to walk – and live his life with a Super Positive Mental Attitude. Life would go on. It did. Everything would be fine. It was.

Ten years passed. Vance was happily married, with a couple of great kids, working, living the good life *of his making*, when he developed high blood pressure. His doctor told him that he needed cardiovascular exercise.

While he had maintained his muscular upper body from walking on crutches, Vance's exercise level was not what it had been and his overall fitness had declined. Vance asked the doctor how he was going to get cardiovascular exercise without the use of his legs.

"Well, you need to get in some races." (Gotta love that doctor!)

"Races?" questioned Vance, "How am I going to do that?"

"There are plenty of wheelchair races now. You should participate."

Vance left the doctor's office without saying anything. He did not want to draw attention to himself by being seen as a "wheelchair guy." But... maybe... well, maybe he could use a wheelchair – just to exercise.

The first time he got in a wheelchair to try it out as "exercise equipment," he just went around his block once – that's one half of a mile. He told me this was the most strenuous exercise he had ever done. The route around his block was slightly uphill for the first half and slightly downhill for the other half.

He was in a regular hospital-type wheelchair at the time. These are wide, heavy, unwieldy contraptions [later he transitioned to a lighter, more agile racing wheelchair]. Maneuvering that kind of chair was extremely difficult and was very hard on his arms and upper body. The second half of the course was a gradual downhill which in order to maintain control of that kind of bulky chair, still took a lot of effort.

It took Vance over twenty minutes to complete the course. He was aching and sore the next day. The difficulty and the pain, however, were not deterrents. He had a fairly profound handicap or disability, but Vance was still Vance. He was back in the chair the next day driven by the same focus, technique, determination and practice that fueled his previous success.

He continued practicing with the awkward, heavy wheelchair until he was able to cut his time in half. He could now get around the block in about ten minutes, still slower than a pedestrian out for a Sunday stroll, but a real accomplishment under the circumstances.

Eventually Vance invested in a better chair and worked up to wheeling a five-mile course. Still not wanting too many people to see him in a wheelchair, he stayed close to home. His five-mile course, therefore, consisted of ten around-the-block loops – each lap taking him about four minutes.

Vance soon took to wheelchair racing. He was, of course, determined to be the best. He brought the same gusto, focus, and determination he had brought to the discus many years before. He spent thousands of hours working out in his wheelchair. Eventually he wheeled a marathon faster than anyone had run it (at the time), averaging just under four minutes and fifty seconds per mile for the twenty-six plus miles of the marathon.

Vance Anderson became known worldwide as a record-setting wheelchair athlete. He set national records at distances from the 5k to the marathon in his category.[5] He also competed in archery, taking fourth place in the National Paralympics. His natural focus and developed upper body strength were significant assets as he added another sport to his repertoire.

Vance has always remained positive. He became a personal counselor and an inspirational speaker. He has spoken several times to my teams over the years, encouraging them to stay on track – especially when the race changes.

His presentation includes playing a guitar and singing his own original songs. One of his songs involves a race where, on a high speed downhill run, the wheel of his chair comes loose, and he crashes. In his best fake country/western accent, he croons…

You picked a fine time to leave me, loose wheel;

Yes, you picked a fine time to leave me, loose wheel…

Vance proved that we can have a super positive attitude and a great sense of humor that keeps us on track, despite (or perhaps because of) the difficult experiences of our lives.

---

5   Categories are determined, in part, by the type of paralysis. For example, Vance is paralyzed from just above the waist down, giving him abdominal strength but he does not have use and strength of his lower back.

Some may have retreated in despair, but Vance used the energy of his challenges to build a great life. He says, "My accident and resulting paralysis may have been the best thing that ever happened to me. I would have been an introvert for the rest of my life if I had not become paralyzed."

6

Farley Gerber

Plan Your Race
and Race Your Plan

No challenge or contest is to be feared. It is only to be understood and prepared for.

~ *Coach Chick Hislop, paraphrasing Marie Curie*

You are the person who has to decide whether you'll do it or toss it aside; You are the person who makes up your mind whether you'll lead or will linger behind; whether you'll try for the goal that's afar; or just be contented to stay where you are.

~ *Edgar A. Guest*

A champion distance runner can't run any further or faster than anyone else, but he plans to anyway.

~ *Brad Barton*

Failing to plan is planning to fail.

~ *(modern version of a Benjamin Franklin quotation)*

The 3000m steeplechase is the only distance event that requires a runner to use a technique other than his running skills.

This event consists of five 36" high 4" thick barriers per lap. Every fifth barrier includes a water jump. That barrier is positioned in front of a twelve-foot- long water pit. The water is eighteen inches deep at the base of the barrier and becomes shallower as it progresses away from the barrier up to the track surface. The runners must clear thirty five barriers during the race, including these seven water jumps.

We worked diligently to advance the runners hurdling ability above and beyond competitors from other schools. I concentrated on developing hurdling skills for the steeplechase because it put us in a competitive position to win.

Julius Korir, a Kenyan[6] running for Washington State University, took second in the steeplechase at the 1983 NCAA Track & Field Championships in Austin, Texas. His time was 8:29. Farley Gerber took fourth in that race with a time of 8:32.

Julius and Farley were the only two in the top eight who would be coming back for the 1984 season.

Farley continued to run in meets during the summer and did very well, improving his time to 8:27.5. He made the national team and participated in the World University Games in Canada where he took second place to a Belgian runner. Farley demolished the American runner who had beaten him earlier at the USA Championships.

We recognized the possibility of his winning the NCAA Championship in the steeplechase in 1984.

About the second or third meet in the spring, we competed at Boise State University. Farley decided to run the 1500m. Julius Korir was there and competed in the 800 meter race. We were sitting on the sideline as we watched Julius run a sensational 1:48. He left his competition far behind, qualifying him for the national meet in the 800m.

---

6   In the 1980's Kenyan runners were recruited by NCAA schools because they dominated the distance events, especially the 3000m steeplechase.

Julius clearly had more speed than Farley. We knew that Farley would not be able to out-sprint him at the end of a race. We needed a plan.

On our five-hour van ride back to Ogden, I was in the passenger's seat. Farley was at the back of the van. After about twenty miles, I heard him say to someone, "Change seats with me," and he moved up behind me.

He sat there quietly for a few minutes, then said, "Coach, what am I going to do? There is no way that I can sprint with Korir. If I try it, he will kick my butt in the last hundred. What can we do? How can I possibly beat him?"

It still gives me goose bumps when I recall how determined this young man was. Even though second in the NCAA, he'd still be the first American because the only person that could beat him was a Kenyan. That wasn't good enough. He was not satisfied to be second to anyone.

He wanted a plan that would put him in position to win. He wanted to be the 1984 NCAA steeplechase champion. Period.

For the next three hours, we discussed possibilities. We talked back and forth about how he could possibly beat Julius Korir. We came to the conclusion that we could not leave it to a finishing kick. The only way we could do it was to attempt to wear Korir down. We needed to see how fast he would finish if we got him tired. Of course, the fallacy in the plan, the Achilles heel, was how to take the kick out of Julius and not kill Farley!

We knew Julius started off faster. We knew he liked to push the pace and then slow down on the penultimate lap about three seconds so he could recover for his outstanding finishing kick. We decided the way for Farley to win was to make Julius run the 3,000m differently than he was used to – to force our opponent to *not* run *his* plan but to run ours. We would bait him to run hard on the next to last lap so he wouldn't have the strength to run a sub-57-second final lap.

Our strategy was to have Farley run a very even pace for five and a half laps (67.5 per lap – that's an 8:28 pace) and then run the last two laps under 62 seconds per lap, running about 2:04 for the final 800 meters. That would make Farley's final time 8:20. We believed that this time would win the race because it was faster than either of their personal bests. We knew that Korir usually ran about a 69 – 57 (2:06) for his last 800, but how fast could he run if he was pushed to run 62 seconds on his next to last lap? We decided to find out.

Our plan was to start every workout at an even pace but run the last part of the workout extremely fast. We started at 400 meters and worked up from there. Before the NCAA meet, Farley would be able to run at least 600 meters at close to a 2:00 minute half-mile pace (or a 4:00 minute mile pace) over barriers at the end of a workout.

We restricted it to 600 meters because we were training at elevation. The meet would be at sea-level. We figured that if he could run a 600m at elevation that he could run an 800m that fast in Eugene, Oregon.

We worked on this plan for eight weeks. We never attempted to run the entire 800 meters. We only did 600 meters. The week before the event, Farley ran a 1:30.2 over barriers for 600 meters at the end of a very hard interval workout. He was ready to race his plan!

As the season progressed, Farley improved incrementally. He ran two hard steeplechases before the NCAA meet. In the first meet, he went hard with 500 meters to go and ran 8:25. In the second meet, he went hard with 600 meters to go and was able to hold the 62-second per lap pace to the finish. Julius Korir and his coach were in the stands. They watched Farley run 8:24 in the second race, beating Julius's teammate.

We did not want them to know that Farley' plan was to accelerate at 800 meters at the NCAA meet.

Going into the meet, Farley Gerber and Julius Korir's season bests in the steeplechase were within two tenths of a second of each other. They had both run 8:24-point-something and were eight seconds better than the third runner.

At the NCAA meet, they had to run trials. They had the two best times, so they were in different sections. In his trial, Julius ran like he always did. He started out fast, slowed down in the middle, then finished fast. He ran in the low 8:30's. He was in excellent shape.

When it was Farley's time to run his trial, the idea was not to run like he was going to in the finals but instead to run as slow as he could while still taking first in his section. About halfway through the race, the excitement finally got to Farley, and he thought, "This is too slow. This is not comfortable." So he picked up the pace.

He too ran in the low 8:30's. The scene was set for the final championship race: an unknown runner from "little ol' 'Webber' State"[7] and a world-ranked Kenyan, a favorite to win the Olympic title.

As the race started the next day, it went according to plan. Julius started out fast and pulled the whole pack with him, except for Farley. Farley stayed with our plan to run the first five-and-a-half laps as evenly and steadily as possible. He knew that if he did that, he would be at the pace he wanted to be with two laps to go. At the end of the first lap, Farley was dead last – about twenty yards behind everyone else. He had to be patient and stick to his plan.

People knew who had the best two times. They also knew who was favored to win. There were some young men sitting in the stands right in front of me.

---

7   Weber State was affectionately called "Little ol' Webber State" by its alumni because it was a small college of about seven thousand students and could afford only a modest athletic program. In addition, when we went to a meet in the eastern part of the country announcers would invariably mispronounce the name "Webber" instead of Weber (WEE-ber).

One of them turned to the other, "Where's Gerber?"

Another pointed out, "He's last."

"He's twenty yards behind everyone, what's *wrong* with him?"

"Yeah, he's living up to his name, Gerber Baby Food."

I thought, "Yeah, if you only knew... Stick with it, Farley. You've planned your race; now race your plan."

He continued on exact pace. He lost ground on the next lap. By the third lap, the pace for the other runners started to slow down. Farley slowly closed the gap between himself and the pack and started passing some of the runners. By the end of five laps, each lap within two tenths of a second of each other, he was in fourth place. The three who were ahead of him were all Kenyan. He was the only American in the lead pack – one lone runner from "little ol' 'Webber' State" and three Kenyans.

By the fifth lap, he had moved up right behind them, but he still had half a lap before he got to the mark where he planned to 'put the pedal to the metal.'

They were easing off the pace a little bit. Instead of taking the lead, Farley waited thirty more meters to get to the point where there were 800 meters – two laps – to go – to the finish.

"Does he have enough courage to follow his plan?" I thought to myself, "If he stays where he is, he will finish second. He'll beat those other two for sure and he'll finish second. If he tries to go, and it doesn't work, he might blow up and may finish fourth."

With a half-mile to go, the finish nowhere in sight, Gerber had to make the decision, "Am I going to go for the win and possibly blow it – and end up fourth? Am I going to put everything on the table?

Or am I going to stay on track and race my plan?" He had planned his race; now it was time to race the plan.

The instant he passed the finish line, he surged. In three steps he was at a 62-second pace, passing the three Kenyans. He was racing his plan! Julius and the other two Kenyans stayed about the same pace. After about 100 meters, Julius realized Farley was serious. He took the bait and sprinted after the American, leaving the other two Kenyans in the dust.

As Farley ran down the backstretch, I heard several spectators say...

"He's miscounted the laps!"

"Farley's going too fast!"

"He thinks he's on his last lap."

"He still has two laps to go! What's he doing?"

Farley started down the home stretch with a little over a lap to go. 17,000 people leaped to their feet clapping rhythmically, chanting, "Gerr-*ber!* Ger-*ber!*..."

Farley Gerber had extended his lead to about twenty meters, with one lap to go. As they started down the backstretch, Julius Korir began to cut into the lead. As they went over the last water jump with about 150 meters to go, Farley's lead had shrunk to eight meters. He executed a perfect water jump. Suddenly his lead was back to twelve meters.

From the last water jump to the last barrier, Julius cut into the lead again. They both had a good last barrier. Farley's eight-meter lead slowly narrowed as they approached the finish line.

Farley held on to win by approximately five meters with a time of 8:19.26. Julius Korir ran 8:19.85. Julius had run a faster last lap than Farley but our plan had worked to perfection.[8]

The remarkable thing about this win was the courage it took to race a plan when there is so much temptation to do otherwise. This can make the difference between being a winner and placing second – or worse.

Planning your race and racing your plan is a mark of a champion. The courage it took at that moment to stay on track and maintain the plan was immense – and it paid off.

Farley crossed the finish line victoriously. The spectators burst into cheering and applause. The Oregon faithful were especially enthusiastic because he had just beaten a Washington State runner. Oregon was in a battle with Washington State for the team title and Gerber had helped Oregon's chances to win.

He took a moment to catch his breath, then Farley took the University of Oregon's traditional victory lap. Watching him take this victory lap was one of my most gratifying experiences as a coach; not just because of the victory it represented, but because I watched him perfectly execute his plan even though he was exhausted.

He had just run the fastest Steeplechase by an American in the history of the NCAA. This American collegiate record stood for twenty-nine years!

After he jogged about 100 meters, the roar of the crowd seemed to revive him. As he passed us about halfway around the track, he put his thumb upwards. We could see a huge grin on his face as if to say, "We did it!" He certainly **planned his race and raced his plan.**

---

8   Competing in the Olympic Games two months later, Julius Korir ran his penultimate lap three seconds slower than his normal race pace then kicked his last lap in 57 seconds, winning the gold.

This kind of planning **works in life as it does on the track**. You have to have a plan. You must believe in it. Then you must put it all on the line, stay on track, and let your plan prove what you can do.

7

Brad Barton

Sacrifice for the Team

Alone we can do so little. Together we can do so much.
~ *Helen Keller*

No person was ever honored for what he received. Honor has
been the reward for what he gave.
~ *Calvin Coolidge*

We often hold the key that unlocks success for others.
~ *Author Unknown*

One man can be a crucial ingredient on a team, but one man
cannot make a team.
~ *Kareem Abdul-Jabbar*

When I first got the job at Weber State, I dreamed of getting a cross
country team qualified for the NCAA meet. Just to have the privilege
of competing at that level would be an amazing achievement for this
small college (now a university).

After two years of dreaming, I got smart. I decided to plan instead of
dream, then create a team that would implement the plan. I changed
"would" into "will" and "if" into "when," transforming my dream
into a goal. I then upped the ante by changing "I" into "we," making

it a team goal.[9] Such is the language of championship teams. That's how we think. That's how we talk.

It *will be* great *when we* qualify for the NCAA meet.

I started to talk to my runners about exactly what we must do, how hard we must work – how we must talk to ourselves and to each other as a team. All of my runners had to up the quality and quantity of their weekly mileage – and improve their track times. Winning locally was not enough. Each team member had to think on a higher level – and also learn to think as a team.

After my two years of dreaming had changed into a year of action, we qualified for the NCAA Cross Country Championships.

As dreams tend to do when they become concrete goals, they enhanced. Our goal now was not just to qualify for the championship, but be a member of the "Sweet Sixteen." The Sweet Sixteen meant the top sixteen cross country teams at the NCAA Championships.

No other team at Weber State had accomplished this on the Division I level. In order to accomplish our goal we had to do all of the things that our past teams had done – and more. I had to recruit more runners with greater talent and work them harder. It was a long-range plan. It took ten years before we had the talent and the experience to reach this goal. Finally, in 1984, we had two runners on the team good enough to be Track & Field All-Americans. We made the "Sweet Sixteen" by taking 11th at the NCAA meet.

Our goal advanced. We set our sights on the "Elite Eight." How could a team, any team, from "little ol' Webber State" even conceive such a dream – much less turn it into a real goal?

In order to reach the Elite Eight, we needed to create a "Magnificent Seven" – a team of seven outstanding runners – including at least

---

9   I wish I could claim credit for this brilliance, but it was taught to me fifteen years earlier by one of my student athletes, Skinny Billy (now Doctor William DeVries).

four "elite runners." (Elite runners are athletes who could become All American.) The workload had to increase because the competition was getting stiffer. Many of the other teams across the nation were bringing in more Kenyans and other accomplished runners from other countries. Our budget restrictions, however, limited our ability to attract top flight runners through scholarships and such. We, therefore, had to rely on local athletes.

By the fall of 1990, I thought we had all the ingredients to make a run at the "Elite Eight." We had seven experienced runners returning – four of them with All-American ability. Our Magnificent Seven were all hard workers and had bought into the idea that we were an Elite Eight team. Two of our seniors, Brad Barton and Bob Durtschi, were both high school state champions. They were also honor roll students and extremely high character athletes. The longer the race, the better Bob was. Brad, however, was mainly a miler.

In cross country, Brad was best at a four-mile race. He could hold his own at five miles. He suffered in the 10K. Both Brad and Bob had qualified for the NCAA track championship. [Brad would become a track All-American the next spring.]

Our four juniors were all solid runners. Brian DeVries and Bret Williams were even better cross country runners than track runners. They loved cross country and excelled at it.

Duane West was dependable and durable at any distance. Possibly the best runner in the junior group was Kurt Black who ultimately became a three-time All-American (See Chapter 9). At that point, Chris Jones, our lone freshman, was probably our most naturally talented runner, ultimately becoming a three-time All-American, but he also needed the most control and direction in a race.

We did, indeed, have the Magnificent Seven required to achieve Elite Eight status. Our Elite Eight dream was now a solid, believable goal. As long as we stayed on track (actually "on course" in cross country), maintaining our team focus and hard work, it was more than believable – it was achievable.

After the first two meets of the season, however, it was obvious we were neither on track nor on course. We simply were not running as well as a team as we should. All seven runners were trying to be number one.

We were racing against each other instead of racing *with and for* each other. In the first race, one runner would push the pace, but if that didn't work out for him personally, he would sit back in the next race. We had no plan – no pattern. In order to compete at the NCAA regional level, we would have to run as a cohesive team instead of seven individuals pitted against each other. The team had to understand that it wasn't just how hard you work that counts, but how you work hard. Turning great runners into a great team required strategy – planning your work and working your plan *as a team*. We had to create a plan and stay on track with it.

After much consideration, I decided to put one runner in charge while they were racing. The other six would have to do exactly what that runner said. I had two choices: Bob or Brad. Both had the respect of the other runners. They would listen to either of them. Bob was likely the strongest runner for the 10K distance at the regionals and the nationals, but it would likely take something out of him if he had to control the other runners.

I decided Brad was my man. His job was to get his teammates to the five-mile mark together and on pace, even if he felt like he was sprinting the last quarter of a mile in order to accomplish this. I told him I didn't care what he did after that. He could just run the last mile with whatever he had left. He could jog in. He could walk in. He could quit (I knew he wouldn't do that). His job was done at the five-mile mark.

This was a major concession to ask of a senior. It did not matter how well he did personally in the last mile. It didn't matter how he looked to the unknowing crowd. What mattered was that he got the *team* to the five-mile mark on-pace and together.

"What if Brad was slow?"

"What if he got off pace?"

"What if he slowed down during the third mile?"

The most asked question from the other runners was, "What if he gets us to the four-mile mark, but we can tell he is fatigued and slowing after that?"

My answer was always the same, "You just rely on Brad and let him manage the race. He'll do the work. You just follow his lead." They could not move ahead of him until the five-mile mark unless I told them specifically otherwise.

The region meet was held at 4600 feet elevation in Salt Lake City. The team knew that if five or six of our guys ran under 31:30 for a 10K (5:03 mile average), we would win.

There were five to seven faster runners from other teams, but they were not on the same team. If we relied on Brad to keep us on track with our plan, it was possible for our top five runners to finish ahead of the second runner from any other team. Going into the meet, the NCAA news had BYU and Weber as a toss-up to win the region championship.

When the race started, most of the other runners started faster than a five-minute mile pace, but Brad brought us through the first mile in a perfectly paced 5:03. At that point, we were quite a ways back (placing somewhere in the 40's) and about fifteen seconds behind the leaders. My instruction from the sideline? "Follow, Brad. He's right on track!"

During the second mile the course kept them out of our view until right before they got to the two-mile mark. They passed the two-mile mark in 10:05. Still at perfect pace! Now as a team, we were in the 30's. BYU's third runner was still about fifteen seconds ahead of us. We were on pace. Their runner must have gone out too fast.

At the three-mile mark, all seven of our runners were right together at 15:09. Brad was an amazing strategist. They had closed the gap on the runners ahead of them, but were still in the 30's, place-wise. BYU's second man was just barely in front of us and their third man was now behind our team.

During the fourth mile, the course again took them away from our view and I could not see them for about three-fourths of that mile. When I could see them again, they had moved into the 20's. As they passed the four-mile mark, I looked at my watch, 20:12. Perfect! Two of our runners looked at me as if to say, "Can we go?

I shouted, "Stay with Brad. He'll do the work. Stay relaxed. Follow Brad."

I shouted encouragement to Brad, "You can do this!"

Brad told me afterwards that he was hoping I would let them go at four miles. But I had confidence in him. I knew that somehow, he would reach the five-mile mark on pace and on time.

I'll always remember those last 100 meters to the five-mile mark. Brad looked like he was sprinting all-out. The other six were within two seconds of him. They passed the five-mile mark in 25:15 exactly on pace. They held the 19th to 25th places as a team.

I yelled, "Go!"

Some pulled away from the others, but none ran a slower last mile. Brad had done his job. He was exhausted, but kept going. It was evident at this point that if the team kept to a five-minute pace, running under 6:15 for the last mile and a quarter, they would win. It was only a matter of by how much.

All six of our runners ran at or under a sub 5-minute last mile. Duane West and Kurt Black finished eighth and ninth overall, running their last mile in 4:45 and 4:46. Chris Jones was eleventh with a 4:50 last mile. Bob Durtschi and Brian DeVries were also under a five-minute pace on their final mile, finishing fourteenth and sixteenth. This gave us a sensational, nearly-unheard-of, thirteen-second split between our first and fifth runners.

All five of our top runners passed at least ten people after Brad got them to the five-mile mark. Bret Williams was close behind in nineteenth, running right at five minutes for his last mile.

Exhausted, Brad had slowed down in the final mile, but he still finished ahead of the fourth man from any other team. We scored fifty-eight points. Northern Arizona came in second with 138 points – eighty points difference (remember, lowest score wins)! We might just be an Elite Eight team.

Brad Barton finished third in the NCAA steeplechase championship the next spring and became an All-American. He went on later in life to do some amazing things as a world class masters runner.[10] His greatest accomplishment, however, was the day he put his personal interests aside and raced his plan to perfection to lead his teammates to the greatest team effort in Weber State history.

Many years later, I was shocked to find out that Brad considered his cross country season a failure. Perhaps now he understands why I have always considered him a champion.

---

10 Teaming up with his old coach, Brad set three Masters (M45-49) World Records: Indoor Mile Run, 4:16.83; Indoor 3000m, 8:26.15; 3000m Steeplechase, 9:06.68; Also set four American Masters records including the M50-54 Outdoor American Record 1500m, 4:01.77. At 48 years old, he became the oldest sub 4:20 miler in world history at 4:17.54.

After our outstanding NCAA regional effort, we traveled to the University of Tennessee to show the nation that we deserved the status of Elite Eight. When we saw the cross country course, I was shocked. The course was extremely hilly. For the entirety of the 6.2 miles the terrain was either up or down. It was never flat. I was not prepared for such a change from the region course. From the looks on their faces my team wasn't either.

That night, at the team meeting, I told my athletes that I knew some of them were better downhill runners and others were better uphill runners. They would have to draw on their own strengths to run well. I did not give them a plan to follow. After they had done such a fantastic job of racing their plan as a team at the region meet, I, in effect, told them they were on their own.

They had prepared and practiced from the beginning of the season to run as a team. Now at the national meet I failed to create a race plan. That was a colossal mistake as a coach. The race was a disaster. It was my fault.

From the start, they got separated from each other and did not know where their team mates were. Durtschi ran up to his potential while the other six runners did not run even close to what they had at the region meet. We ended up with a 1:15 second split between our first and fifth runners. Our top runner at the recent region meet was not among our top five in the national meet.

We went into the meet knowing we were an Elite Eight team, but we didn't perform as such. We finished 14th. Even though being in the top sixteen was a coveted position, it was a long silent trip home as we smarted over the humiliation of being dropped to a "Sweet Sixteen" team. Sweet Sixteen is not so sweet when you know you are better than that.

The team did as well as they could under the circumstances. In fact, they had accomplished something that Weber State had never before accomplished. They had placed higher than any other sport in our college had in an NCAA championship meet. The team and I were disappointed in what we felt was a sub-par performance because we knew that we could have done better. Actually, I could have done better. I did not create a winning plan for them.

If I had a chance to do this again, I would do what I did at the regional meet, except I'd have released them at the four-mile mark, instead of the five. The team would have raced the plan, stayed together, and solidified our place as an Elite Eight team.

Lesson learned. Don't let your environment control you. Winning requires you to consistently control your environment.

The course had unnerved me. I did not follow my own advice, create a plan and stick to it. I let the challenging cross country course control my thoughts and knock me and, consequently, my team, off track.

In order to correct a mistake, you must first admit that you made a mistake. I had not only made a mistake, I had made a whopper! From then on, every team I coached would have a race plan and definite instructions on how to race that plan – as a *team*.

8

Weber State's 1991 Cross Country Team

Yesterday's Problem Creates Today's Plan

Plan ahead...It wasn't raining when Noah built the ark.
~ *Cardinal Richard Cushing*

If I had eight hours to chop down a tree, I'd spend six sharpening my axe.
~ *Abraham Lincoln*

Failure is only a temporary change in direction to set you straight for your next success.
~ *Denis Waitley*

Confidence is belief in ourselves. Charisma is belief in our team.
~ *Thomas Cantrell*

On the long silent ride home from the 1990 NCAA Cross Country championship, I began to plan for the next cross country season. Five of our top seven runners would be coming back. Our team needed at least one other runner that could step in and run with the returning five. We also had to get some of the returning five to a higher level of running.

It was time to stop worrying about our setbacks and realize the value in the experience. Remember, last year's problem outlines this year's plan. Besides, planning is half the fun of getting there.

Early in the recruiting process, I found Nathan Kennedy, a high school runner from Evanston Wyoming. He had outstanding track times, but no cross country experience whatsoever. He had been running about twenty five miles a week in high school, while our guys were running between sixty and eighty miles a week.

When he came for a recruiting visit, I told him his track times were impressive but what I really needed was a cross country runner. He could receive financial help from us if he would commit to getting his mileage up to at least sixty miles a week during the summer. He agreed.

Nathan worked harder that summer than any incoming freshman I have ever coached. By the middle of August he was running sixty quality miles a week. We had to be careful not to break him down, though, so now we had to level him off.

During the spring track season, Chris Jones, Brian DeVries and Kurt Black took my challenge to race at a higher level and advanced to the next level of competition.

As the fall cross country season began, they were running better than the year before. Three others, Duane West, Bret Williams and Nathan Kennedy were running about the same or a little behind where our fourth, fifth and sixth runners were the year before. As the season progressed, Bret Williams suffered an injury followed by illness and was, therefore, not running as well has he had the previous year. We had to rely on Nathan Kennedy, our freshman, to be our fifth man.

This team was unique in the NCAA. Six of our athletes were born and raised primarily in Utah and educated in Utah schools for some, if not all, of their careers. Our seventh, Frank Fox, was a Big Sky caliber runner, but he wasn't yet at the level that would help us in a national meet. Chris Jones, Kurt Black, Brian DeVries, and Bret Williams had gone to high school within fifteen miles of Weber State's campus. Duane West went to elementary school in Clearfield, Utah (about ten miles from Weber State) before his parents moved to Boise, Idaho where he attended high school. Nathan Kennedy, our freshman, had gone to school in St. George, Utah through the eighth grade. His father, who worked for the Forest Service, moved the family to Oregon for his ninth and tenth grade years then to Evanston, Wyoming for his final two years of high school.

Our first significant meet that year was the prestigious Roy Griak Cross Country Invitational in Minnesota. This competition was named after the University of Minnesota's legendary cross country coach.

We started out the season poorly, finishing in seventh place. The University of Wisconsin, who had an outstanding coach in Martin Smith and runners from all over the United States, finished in sixth place just ahead of us. When the race was over, I was standing next to Martin. Both of us had long faces.

Roy Griak came up to us and asked, "What happened? It looks like you guys just lost your best friend."

I replied, "Well I might be standing next to my best friend as far as coaching is concerned, but our teams certainly didn't perform up to their potential this afternoon."

Our teams had established plans but were not sold on them so they did not execute them as they should have.

On the phone after the meet, Martin and I assured each other that, even though our respective teams had not done what they were capable of that day we would meet again at the NCAA meet.

As a member of the NCAA Track & Field Rules Committee, I had to attend the Pre-National NCAA meet designed to help coaches, athletes and officials get acquainted with the course before the National competition in Tempe, Arizona.

My plan was to take my team with me to give them another opportunity to experience the course.

After their performance in Minnesota, however, I decided that workouts were more important than racing at this point in the season. At that time, there were only four at-large teams that could be picked by the committee to attend the NCAA National Championships in addition to the teams who automatically qualified out of the District competitions. Even if our team performed well at the Pre-Nationals, I was not sure that we would be selected as an at-large team, so I elected to have our team stay home and work.

I went alone to Arizona to represent the Rules Committee and to check out the course. I needed to make sure it was suitable and recommend changes, if necessary.

The altitude of Tempe is about 2400 feet which is a little below the NCAA allotment in terms of altitude time-conversion. The course itself, however, was situated about fifteen miles outside of town toward the foothills at an elevation of 3200 feet.

The race started at the highest point on the course and was flat for about 400 meters. The course then angled downhill for about 1200 meters. The runners would finish the race at this lowest point, after two and a half laps.

For the first two laps, the runners would pass this area and run through six-inch deep dry sand for a 100m stretch followed by a turn and a dramatic uphill – possibly the steepest hill I have ever seen on an NCAA national cross country course. The steep uphill portion extended for four hundred meters, where it became more gradual, then continued for another three quarters of a mile as the athletes made their way back up to the race's starting elevation.

Running this two and-a-half-mile loop and a shorter flatter 1000m section – twice – comprised the 10K *national* course.

Because the *pre-national* race distance was set at 8K, they modified the course from the 10K route described above. The course remained the same for the first lap, but the second lap cut off the steep portions, so the athletes did not have to run up the brutally steep hill twice. All the coaches seemed satisfied with the modification. They felt that given the single uphill the terrain was not too difficult for the five-mile Pre-Nationals.

I spent many hours over the next few weeks on the phone with Coach Smith planning how to run the difficult 10K course. While the times in the Pre-National did not reflect a difficult course, I felt that adding a second steep uphill and sandy section would make the national course much more difficult. The athletes would have to be very careful not to go out too fast. In the Pre-National, the front-runners opened up their first mile of the race in the low 4:20's. We knew it would kill our runners if they went out that fast for the 10K course.

Over the next month, we continued to discuss our team strategy in handling the unique characteristics of this course. We knew it would be a faster first mile because it was downhill, but we agreed that we could not get carried away. The first mile had to be "comfortable," which meant finding a balance between a restrained and a lengthened downhill stride. If taken to an extreme, either would cause fatigue later in the race.

The best way for us to prepare for this event was to find terrain in Ogden that mirrored the first mile of the course where we could do weekly downhill mile repeats. The athletes would learn to feel the appropriate stride and effort that was needed for that first mile of the

Tempe course. During these days, I was careful to have the men run hard downhill (but under control) and not turn and run hard back up the hill. Instead we could take a short cut back to the start of the downhill mile. The men would walk/jog this shorter distance as a recovery "lap" and then do another downhill mile repeat.

We knew we were not going to receive one of the coveted four at-large bids, so we had to place in the top two in our respective districts in order to get an automatic bid to the national meet.

Over the course of the season, our Weber State team divided themselves into two groups. Black, DeVries and Jones ran together in the first group. The second group consisted of West, Kennedy, Bret Williams and Frank Fox.

In practice these groups worked out together.

Bret had not recovered from his injuries well enough to run with the other two through the entire race but, because of his teammates' inexperience, it was Bret's job to pace West and Kennedy for the first four miles. His job was like Brad Barton's the year before. His objective was to manage the race, prevent them from going out too fast and to keep them together at a pace they could handle.

Our seventh runner, Frank Fox was to run with the second pack and help them as long as possible. I continually stressed the importance of running together in the District and National meets, and not repeat the debacle of last year. Our goal was to have them run in their respective groups within touching distance of one another for the first four miles. The first group would run each mile about five seconds faster than the second group. This would give us a forty second split between the first and the fifth runner – which was respectable on a national level.

For five weeks the team practiced this plan on tempo runs, on easy runs, and during interval workouts. Our athletes' disciplined ability to execute the plan brought them an outstanding victory. They won the district meet by seventeen points – and qualified us for the NCAA Cross Country.

This team wasn't quite as talented as the previous year's squad, but they were proving to be much better prepared for the nationals than our last year's team. Running the race and knowing the pace is important. Of special importance with this particular course, was to prepare the runners for a fast opening mile.

If they ran 4:35 – 4:40 for the first mile, they would be fast enough, but it also meant they would be approximately twenty seconds behind the leaders, who I was sure would go out in a sub 4:20 first mile. They should be able to pick off some runners who had gone out too quickly on the first hill and maintain position as they completed the first loop. Staying steady into the second loop, down the hill, and into the sand would allow them the reserve energy necessary to take the steep hill the second time as fast as they did the first time and pass runners who were fatiguing from their too-quick opening mile.

Coach Martin Smith and his Wisconsin athletes would approach the race with a similar strategy. His scholarship-recruited runners were a little more talented than mine, but they too were planning a conservative first loop. They would likely be behind the main pack but ahead of us during the first loop.

Wisconsin's goal was to make the "Final Four."

Ours was to finish in the "Elite Eight."

After the district meet we were ranked 14th in the coach's poll. This was about right, given our finish the previous year. Our team knew we should have been higher the year before, and this ranking was encouraging after our relatively poor showing at the Griak Invitational.

Three days before the NCAA meet – between the District and

National meets – Kurt Black came into my office and said, "Coach, I'm not sure that I can go to the National meet."

"What! You can't?"

"The doctor just told my family today that Dad has less than a week to live, and I want to be here when he passes."

"Well, Kurt, yes, I understand. You really should be with your dad."

The next day, Kurt came back and, with a slight smile, said "Coach, I am going to run after all."

"Why?"

"Well, Dad told me two things. First, he said I should go. Second, he promised he would still be alive when I get home."

So it was that we left for the national meet with injuries and a heavy heart. We also had hope. We had planned our race and now we were headed to Arizona prepared and determined to race our plan.

We went over the course the day before the meet. Recognizing how difficult the course was, my athletes were even more determined to stay on track with the plan we had practiced.

We had scheduled a team meeting that night. Our athletic director, Dick Hannon, wanted to know if it was okay for him to attend. During that meeting we reviewed our plan in detail. The runners were to start off conservatively, run the first loop comfortably. They would likely be close to the back but, as the race went on, they would continue to improve their positioning. They just had to remain patient and not move up too quickly.

"Run in your groups and stick to the plan," I cautioned, "The real race begins when you start up the hill for the *second* time."

At the end of the meeting, the athletes brought out some special Weber State T-shirts. "Coach, is it okay if we wear these during the warmup tomorrow?"

I looked at the shirts and chuckled. "Yes, if you want to wear 'em that will be fine."

On the back they had a group photo of the seven runners with the words, "Locally Grown," above the picture and "Nationally Known" below the picture.

They were proud of the fact that they were all from Utah. Only three had even received a recruiting phone call from any another coach, and only two had actually taken a recruiting visit to another school. The others were not recruited by anyone else but me. They were proud of the fact that they were, indeed, "Locally Grown and Nationally Known."

After the team meeting, our athletic director told me he had never been to a cross country meeting before and asked if I really expected the team to follow the tightly disciplined plan we had discussed.

I replied, "If the plan is right, they follow it … so, yes, they will stay on track with *this* plan. You watch and see."

The weather was perfect the morning of the race. It was warm, but not too warm for a November day in Arizona. As the gun sounded, most of the field sprinted out to get a good position before making the turn and heading down the hill. I was on the top of the hill looking down at the first mile mark. My prediction was a little off. The pack went out *way* too fast. The leaders actually clocked their first mile in 4:12! The entire pack was already passing this point when my watch read 4:20.

Our Weber State runners were last at 4:36 – 4:38. Wisconsin was just a little ahead of us. There were only a few individual stragglers lagging behind us.

The pack hit the turn just after the first mile and headed up the hill. Following behind, steady and on pace, were Wisconsin's red uniforms and Weber State's purple jerseys. As they crested the hill on the first lap, Weber had passed about thirty runners. Our team was still behind the big pack but we were no longer the last group. As my team passed me, I shouted encouragement, *"Stay relaxed! Stay on pace! C'mon! Race your plan!"*

If they would race the plan and just stay on pace, the runners that went out too fast would fatigue as the race progressed, and our team would gain position.

I cut across a cactus and sagebrush field to get back to the starting point so I could see where the runners were placed as they completed the first loop. They had picked up a few places, but were maintaining position – running exactly as we had planned and practiced. Our first group of three was about ten seconds ahead of our second group of three. Bret had managed his part of the race perfectly. We were now approaching the four mile mark on pace.

I now needed to get to a spot on the course where I could count positions and see where my runners were in the pack. I made my way to the portion of the course where the steep hill became a more gradual rise. If we had anyone within the top fifty runners, we had a good chance to place in the Elite Eight.

I started counting: thirty … thirty-one … thirty-two … thirty-three … thirty-four … Three runners passed tightly bunched, then thirty-eight…thirty-nine… I strained to see further back down the course – trying to locate our runners. Then it dawned on me…

I turned to my right and looked again at the runners that had just passed me. I realized that thirty-five, thirty-six, and thirty-seven were *our* runners! They were running side by side. In just three quarters of a mile, they had passed almost one hundred runners. I was so excited… but they had already passed me, and I had missed my opportunity to tell them what a great job they were doing.

At that point I was busy trying to recount runners so that I could determine the positioning of our second pack. As they passed me, Duane and Nathan were running side by side in 91st and 92nd place.

I waited for Bret to reach me so I could encourage him. Then I rushed back across the cactus and sagebrush field to get to the five-mile mark in time to check on my other runners. They told me later that this field, which I ran across several times that day, was prime habitat for rattlesnakes. This explains why I was the only one running back and forth across the field!

I made some quick calculations and determined our current score to be right around 300 points. That should place us among the top ten teams. We had a good chance to reach our goal. When the runners passed me at the five-mile mark, I told them they were now on their own; they could pick up the pace if they felt they could; they no longer needed to run as a group.

When the runners from the second group passed, I yelled, "We'll be in the top ten. We *will* be in the top ten." Then I took off for the finish line – through the sagebrush-laden snake-infested field.

Some of the runners had already finished by the time I arrived. I saw a runner racing down the hill, arms flailing wildly in every direction to keep his balance as he blew past several other runners. It was Chris Jones! Not far behind him were Brian DeVries and Kurt Black. That rounded out our first pack of three. I couldn't determine their places at the finish, but our next two runners came in just as strong. In the last mile, they had all passed several of the best cross country runners in the nation. After the race, they converged on me, "What place are we, Coach?"

Not knowing exactly, I said, "Well… I *think* we are in the Elite Eight."

Chris Jones said excitedly, "I *know* we are in the Elite Eight!"

"Chris, you were in front of everybody else, how would you *know* that?"

"I just know, Coach!"

Because I was on the NCAA Rules Committee, I could get into the results area and see the outcome before it was announced. I was certain Arkansas had won the meet and that Iowa State was likely second (both teams were comprised mostly of foreign athletes). As I walked by, the Michigan coach asked, "Coach, how did you do?"

I was cautiously optimistic. "Well, I think we may be in the top ten."

"Yes, I think you are; because I am pretty sure you beat us and I'm certain *we* are in the top ten," he replied.

His comment brought a hopeful smile to my face. I walked by Coach Smith and asked him how he felt his Wisconsin team had fared. He said, "I think we made the top five." My optimism spiked. I knew we weren't too far behind Wisconsin. In fact, our top three had finished ahead of their fourth and fifth runners.

As I approached the results area, my athletic director, Dick Hannon, ran up behind me. He was so excited and winded that I could barely understand him, "That was great!" he puffed, "I can't believe it! Your runners did exactly what you talked about last night. Talk about 'race your plan.' It was as if all the other runners just let our guys do what they were supposed to do."

Touched by his excitement, I grinned. "Well, that's one way to look at it!" He was right. Our team had doggedly stuck to the plan and did not let the field pull them off pace.

In the results area, I watched the officials writing the names on the board – in those days they still wrote team results on a chalkboard.

They had recorded teams 6-10 on one board and teams 1-5 on the other. I didn't realize that the top five had already been written and the board they were writing on was covering the first board. I watched them write out:

6th place: Michigan
7th place: Texas
8th place: Tennessee
9th place: Michigan State
10th place: Penn State

Not seeing Weber State, I thought, "Oh no! What happened? Where are we?"

I looked again. I hadn't realized that after they had written the tenth team, they had switched the boards back again so that the board reflecting the first five teams was on top. Arizona was fifth. I could barely contain my emotions. We were fourth!

We had achieved the Final Four. Wisconsin was third. Iowa State was second. Arkansas was first.

I walked out of the results area trying my best to suppress my excitement. I couldn't let anyone see my reaction because the results had not yet been officially released.

I saw my son, Lance, about fifty yards away. He mouthed, "What place are we?" I held up four fingers and mouthed back, "Fourth." He looked surprised and held up one finger on one hand and four fingers on the other, "Fourteenth?"

Shaking my head, "No," I again mouthed, *"Fourth!"* I placed my finger to my lips, "Shhhhhhhh…"

Lance understood what we had accomplished. He, too, was overcome with joy but forced to contain it until the results were official. When they were finally announced, I was engulfed by a thrilled, excited group of winners!

We had surpassed our goal of being in the Elite Eight. We had landed in the Final Four. Weber State's first Division One NCAA trophy! As of this writing, this trophy still stands as Weber State's most impressive athletic accomplishment.

This was definitely a highlight of my coaching career; not so much because of how high we had placed but because our athletes that year fulfilled their individual tasks – doing their personal best and thereby achieving a team victory – an all-time school best. They knew what was expected of them. They planned their race. They raced their plan. They won for themselves, for their team, and for their school.

Their final places were as follows:

Chris Jones: 22nd
Brian DeVries: 27th
Kurt Black: 32nd

I don't remember between Duane West and Nathan Kennedy who was 77th or 78th but they finished together, within a tenth of a second of each other.

As I said before, based on our place values at the five-mile mark, we had approximately 300 points. We ended up scoring 236 points. That means we improved our position by over 60 points late in the race.

On average, each of our runners passed twelve other competitors over the final 1.2 miles of the course. Everyone did an outstanding job that morning, once again proving that in athletics, as in business and in life, you must have a plan; then you must stay on track to execute that plan. Regardless of your circumstances or environment; regardless of what is going on around you – or within you – you must see it through.

When the race was over, I asked my athletes, "How did you pass so many runners – going up the hill – for the second time?"

Kurt Black replied incredulously, "Coach, you were right. You would not believe how many were *walking* up that hill; even in a national championship – they were *walking!* They had gone out way, *way* too fast."

After examining the official results more closely, I noticed that several of the runners who were among the top twenty-five in the race when they passed me at the three-mile mark ended up finishing behind our fourth and fifth runners. What made the difference? Our team had planned our race and did not let our competition pull us off pace.

Kurt Black's father kept his promise. He was still in this world to proudly congratulate his son and his team when they returned with their trophy.

He passed away two days later.

9

Kurt Black

Outside Your Comfort Zone

Excellence is never an accident.
> ~ *Aristotle*

That which we persist in doing becomes easier to do; not that
the nature of the thing has changed, but that our ability to do
has increased.
> ~ *Ralph Waldo Emerson*

Mentally tough competitors are disciplined thinkers.
> ~ *Dr. James E Lochr*

Kurt Black was a good distance runner; however, when he started to
do hurdle drills it was obvious that he could become an outstanding
steeplechaser.

When I started coaching at Weber State I realized I could take a good
distance runner and make him into an outstanding steeplechaser by
perfecting his hurdle skills. A runner who could place in the mile
could be All Conference in the steeple. If he could be All Conference
in a flat race, he could be first or second in the steeple when he
developed his hurdling. If he could qualify for nationals in the
1500m he could be an All American in the steeple chase by having
the best hurdling skills of anyone in the race.

Weber State distance runners would always be one level higher in the steeple than they would be in a flat race. I emulated a great coach from South High School Coach Nate Long who made outstanding hurdlers from good sprinters.

It takes much dedicated work, of course, on technique and skill to perfect distance runners' hurdling. It also takes a steady dose of repetition over a long period of time.

As Kurt worked on his hurdling technique, it became apparent that he had a considerable imbalance between his hips. He could hurdle much better leading with his left leg than his right. He had good flexibility and was able to execute all of his steeplechase drills with his left leg, but the muscle balance was not there in his right hip so he could not get into appropriate hurdling position on that side.

We worked on this for some time achieving only small gains. He decided to work on strengthening the other leg so that he was strong enough to be higher over the hurdle, trailing his weak leg slightly beneath him, instead of extending it out to his side where the trail leg should be. After four years of work, he had become strong enough so that there was negligible difference between his hurdling efficiency with both legs, despite the difference in height with which he had to clear the hurdles.

Those four years of working through his hurdling challenges gave Kurt the experience of aiming for perfection the hard way – stepping out of his comfort zone, and choosing to take a longer, more arduous path aimed at perfection. The comfort zone is never comfortable – for a champion.

In 1993, at the beginning of Kurt's senior season, it was obvious that the NCAA steeplechase race would be contested between four seniors: Donavan Bergstrom of the University of Wisconsin; Jim Svenoy, a Dutchman from the University of Texas El Paso; Francis O'Neil, Kansas State; and Kurt Black, Weber State. All four had placed in the top six in the NCAA Championships the previous year.

Bergstrom, Svenoy, and O'Neil had all achieved a sub four-minute mile. Kurt's personal best mile, however, was a comparatively plodding 4:12.

What could we do over the next eight months to overcome the other three athletes' leg speed and get Kurt a solid chance of winning the 1993 NCAA Steeplechase title?

Knowing the coaches from the other schools – knowing their athletes' typical patterns of racing – we knew that Kurt needed to lead the race to keep the pace from going too slow. If the race started slowly, Kurt would struggle as the pace quickened to a kicker's final sprint. We needed to create a new comfort zone for Kurt. He needed to build his confidence in leading races.

He had to break free from his comfort zone of following. He needed to remain consistent and focused – and force other runners out of their comfort zones by making them race *his* plan...

Our plan was for Kurt to lead every steeplechase he would run that spring. It was critical that he doggedly race this plan at every meet. This would prepare him to apply the same strategy at the NCAA meet.

Kurt practiced this strategy in all of his workouts. He never let his teammates pace him in any of his hard steeplechase workouts. Sometimes he intentionally ran alone.

Before the 1993 season, Kurt's best time in the steeplechase was 8:39. Our goal was to have him run faster than that as many times as he could before the collegiate national championship. We wanted him to clock at least an 8:34 before the national meet.

When we traveled from Utah to a sea level race, Kurt would execute this plan. He would take the lead within the first lap forcing a quick pace early in the race. He would run the remaining laps as evenly as possible.

He maintained this strategy in our conference meet. The steeplechase was the leadoff event. Kurt won in 8:38 only to come back later that evening to run the 10000 Meters and the following day to run the 5000 Meters.

Critics were plentiful. I was told that I was working Kurt too hard – not just throughout the season, but also in our conference championship. Were they right? Were we pushing it? We really didn't know, but that was our plan. We felt the preparation was necessary to achieve our goal of running a successful qualifying time in the trials and then, two days later, going after the NCAA title.

This plan forced Kurt to expand his comfort zone by forcing his competition out of their comfort zones for the first time in their running careers.

By the time Kurt arrived at the national meet, he had established a steeple time of 8:35.5. This was a faster time, by about four seconds, than Bergstrom, Svenoy, and O'Neil had run thus far.

They had won races during the season by tucking in behind other athletes and kicking past them in the final laps. They had never led or pushed the pace during the early stages of the race. Kurt had.

The season had gone as expected. The four athletes who were expected to run well showed up to contend for the steeplechase title – with one addition: a Kenyan from the University of Arizona, Martin Keino. He had also run well during the outdoor season. His best time was second only to Kurt. All five advanced to the NCAA finals, as expected. There were now five top athletes vying for the national title.

The gun went off to start the steeplechase final. Kurt took the lead within the first 200 meters. The others were content to tuck in and follow. Kurt moved out at a steady pace with the intent of running under 8:30. The race continued at that pace for over five laps; then, with two laps to go, Kurt quickened the pace slightly.

Unaccustomed to such a quick pace for the first laps, Martin Keino, faded back. Halfway through the sixth lap, Jim Svenoy took the lead and pushed the pace. For the first time, Kurt relaxed a little bit and followed Svenoy. With just over 300 meters to go, Bergstrom made a quick move from the back and took the lead. O'Neil tried to follow. The four runners took the last water barrier virtually side by side. That was an amazing sight!

Bergstrom had a slightly better water jump, emerging from the pit just ahead of the other three. Going into the last barrier, O'Neil stutter-stepped to take the hurdle with his preferred leg and fell slightly behind.

The first three athletes finished within .17 of a second, a closer finish that the 110 high hurdles earlier that day. Bergstrom won the race (8:29.08); Svenoy was second (8:29.18); Kurt Black came in third (8:29.25); O'Neil finished fourth (8:29.64).

Keino was not able to respond to the surges of the others. He finished ten seconds behind.

Was Kurt Black's race plan successful? He did not "win." He ended up third. But he did so against three sub-four-minute milers whose personal bests Kurt's leadership enhanced.

His plan was, therefore, eminently successful.

By expanding his comfort zone, by leading the race and pushing the pace, he not only achieved his personal best, he also moved the others out of their comfort zones. If Kurt had not run his plan it is likely that he would have been out-kicked by a much greater distance and would have finished no higher than fourth.

More importantly, because of Kurt's strategy, *all four* athletes ran their personal best that afternoon.

When real leaders win, everyone wins.

The true success of this strategy was revealed two weeks later, when Kurt competed at the USA Championship Meet. At the time, I was on the NCAA Rules Committee. We had a meeting that conflicted with the first night of the steeplechase, so I was unable to watch Kurt run in the trials. Kurt called me when it was over saying that he had just barely made it into the finals. He told me that he felt tired, drained, and had only run an 8:38. He qualified, but it was one of his slowest times of the year.

I asked Kurt what the other NCAA athletes had run. When he told me they ran in the 8:36s, I told him not to worry. We would come up with a plan to stay on track.

When I arrived in Eugene the following morning, Kurt's mindset had improved. He claimed he felt better, but he commented on how "heavy" he felt during the trials race. I assured him that this was normal. He had just run two taxing races at the NCAA meet less than a week earlier. He was experiencing some mental letdown from the length and intensity of the season. When the race the previous evening didn't feel right, he experienced an emotional drain (probably because he had thought that getting into the finals of this competition would be fairly easy).

I warned Kurt that he would likely feel fatigued during the first three laps of the finals race, just as he had in the trials; but if he would stick with his plan and maintain focus, he would start to feel better, and would probably have the best race of his life.

Kurt gave me a puzzled look. "You really believe that Coach?"

I said, "Absolutely! If you approach the race with a positive mindset and mental focus, you will be able to run a little out of your new comfort zone and achieve another personal best."

There were three professional runners competing in this race: Mark Croghan and Mark Davis who previously won national championships. Brian Diemer was an Olympic medalist.

Croghan and Davis went out fast and immediately vied for the lead. Brian Diemer followed closely. For the first time all year, Kurt did not have to lead. He was able to relax and feel the race unfold.

We did not worry about exact times because I knew the caliber of the field and felt that the race would go out quickly enough. I didn't want Kurt to be concerned about his lap pace; rather, I wanted him to be willing to do what he had done all year, just push a little and get out of his comfort zone.

Kurt helped me realize that working outside of your comfort zone involves setting realistic goals. If the tasks are realistic though perhaps difficult, it becomes much easier to remain energized and focused in workouts and races, or in life.

That's how you improve. That's how you win.

As the race progressed, the two leaders opened a significant gap. The remainder of the pack, led by Brian Diemer, maintained a steady pace – until Diemer went after the leaders. That spread the group out. With a lap to go, Kurt had moved into sixth place, about fifteen meters behind Diemer. At the 400 mark Kurt got bumped by another runner and was knocked off the track. This got his adrenaline going and he got back on track and began to sprint. He realized he had more energy than ever to finish a race. He passed two runners and closed on Diemer.

He came in fourth in the USA Championships. He lost to Diemer by less than a second, while achieving a new personal record of 8:23.52, about six seconds faster than his NCAA third place finish.[11]

---

11 What happened to Bergstrom and O'Neil? When these athletes were forced to race someone else's plan, fatigue caught up with them. They were not prepared to run outside their comfort zone a second time. After winning the NCAA Championship, Donovan Bergstrom suffered general fatigue and leg pain and was unable to compete in the USA finals. Francis O'Neil competed, but finished in eighth place at 8:37.

10

Wiley King

From the Edge of Defeat

Adversity causes some men to break; others to break records.
~ *William A. Ward*

A diamond is a bit of coal that did well under pressure.
~ *Thomas Cantrell*

Only a mediocre person is always at his best.
~ *W. Somerset Maugham*

Every adversity, every failure, every heartache carries with it the seed of an equivalent or greater benefit.
~ *Napoleon Hill*

Weber State University's football coach invited Wiley King, an outstanding football player from Portland, Oregon, for a recruiting visit. The head coach asked me to interview Wiley because he had said he wanted to attend a college where he would be able to participate in track & field as well as football.

Wiley's decision to attend Weber State was partly made for him. He had gotten mixed up with the wrong crowd and into some trouble his senior year of high school, so some coaches from other colleges had become less interested in him.

When he arrived at Weber in the fall, the assistant football coaches convinced him that it would be difficult to earn and maintain his position if he split his time with track.

Then they red-shirted him so he would still have four years of NCAA eligibility after developing his skills during his freshman year.

Two months later, after the indoor track season had begun, he still had not come out for the track team. I assumed the assistant coaches had convinced him to concentrate on football.

One day he walked into my office saying, "Coach, I would like to come out for track."

I was somewhat surprised, but I told him that he was welcomed to try out.

I had to gain permission from the football coach, Jerry Graybeal, to let Wiley run track because he was on a Weber State football scholarship.

Coach Graybeal informed me that Wiley had not done well with his academic studies; therefore, Wiley should concentrate on his studies and not run track. I promised him that if he would let Wiley come out for track, I would see to it that we would never again have to worry about Wiley's grades.

"Okay..." Graybeal shrugged.

When Wiley stopped attending the football team's mandatory three times a week study hall, Coach Graybeal came to me with great concern. "What is going on? Wiley is missing study hall!"

I replied, "Not really. He is studying at my house two hours a night every week-day."

He said, "Oh, good!" He walked away.

For the rest of Wiley's freshman year, he would wait for me to finish my coaching, ride home with me, study for two hours – actually study – without the interruption of television or stereo.

Wiley made the Dean's list with a GPA of 3.5 his junior year and went on to earn his master's degree.

Later I found out *why* Wiley had decided to join the track team.

The freshman football players' locker room was directly across from the track locker room, separated by two pillars, but no wall. One day, some of the freshman offensive lineman were talking loudly and boisterously demeaning women in vulgar terms (indeed, they were "offensive" linemen).

Wiley was in the room when one of our distance runners, Jeremy Tolman, three time NCAA Track & Field All American, walked over and asked them to change their vocabulary. He said, "We shouldn't have to sit in our locker room and listen to this kind of stuff."

Three lineman, each nearly twice Jeremy's size, confronted him in a threatening manner. "We don't have to change anything. The way we talk is none of your business."

Unintimidated, Jeremy shot back, "I'll make it my business. I'll talk to coaches, the athletic director; whoever I have to. We don't have to listen to that kind of language."

With vulgar expletives thrown in for effect, the lineman demanded to know why Jeremy had the right to tell them how to behave.

"When you win as many championships in football as we have in track, maybe we'll follow your example. Until then, you can follow ours."

The football players had nothing else to say.

Overhearing this exchange, Wiley realized which team was most important to him. "As I listened to Tolman," Wiley said, "I could see that he was not going to back down – no matter how big the other guys were. I decided then and there I had to be a part of his team."

Wiley wanted to associate with high-class student athletes – not just jocks. Wiley joined the track team because of their team culture. Wiley truly became a part of the track environment. He found closer and better friendships there.

It didn't take long before the football players started respectfully referring to him as "The Track Man."

As our outdoor conference meet approached, I realized it was going to be a tight competition. We had a shot at the Big Sky Conference title; however, all the close races would have to tip in our favor for us to pull off a team victory.

One of the reasons we always did well in our conference meets was because every athlete knew exactly what he had to do – exactly where he had to place – in order for us to win the meet as a team. If an athlete had to win a first place, fourth place, or fifth place in his event – I'd tell him so. Everyone went into every meet knowing how many points they had to individually score to achieve a team victory.

Going into this particular meet, we needed Wiley to score eighteen points. We knew he could score in the long jump, the high jump, and the high hurdles. There was another event I thought he may be able to score in: the triple jump.

Although Wiley's best mark was about five feet shorter than the best jumper in the triple jump, I decided to enter him in that event on the chance that he could maybe earn us a point. The triple jump was the last event he would compete in. It was a good strategy. If we didn't need him, we could scratch him. If we did need him, he would have already completed in his other events.

I also decided to take a freshman, Bret Ferrier, off his red-shirt year and use his eligibility to run the 10000m. I thought that he could score at least one or two points, so he went to the meet to run the first 10K of his life – in a conference championship!

One of the first events was the men's long jump. In the long jump, the athlete has three attempts to get a legal jump in the trials round. The top eight get three additional jumps and a chance to score in the meet. We expected Wiley to take second place – which would give us eight points.

On his first jump, Wiley's steps were off and he scratched. His second jump was also a scratch by about six inches. It came down to his third and final attempt. We moved him back about a foot on the runway to give him plenty of space. Wiley charged down the runway, hit the board and landed way out in the pit at about the 24-foot mark. We were excited, thrilled... Then we saw the judge raise a red flag. Wiley had gone over the board by about ¼ of an inch and was out of the competition.

As soon as he saw the red flag go up, Wiley dropped his arms and his head in despair. He did not get angry. He did not question the call. He just went to the edge of the track and sat down. I could see his upper body start to shake. I jumped the fence, which I was not supposed to do, and ran over to him. I put my arm around him.

"Are you okay?"

He put his head on my shoulder, "Coach, I let you down," he sobbed. "I let the team down." He couldn't seem to stop crying.

The people around the long jump pit fell stone silent. I walked Wiley around the corner of the stands so he would not be the center of attention. I tried to talk him through his despair. I got him to move around a bit.

As a coach there are some times when it's appropriate to express frustration toward an athlete. This was not one of those times. The best course of action was to console Wiley and get him moving again, physically and mentally.

After about fifteen minutes, I told him I had to go check on some of his teammates. I asked him if he was okay. He said he was. I had sent one of the other athletes to get his shoes and before I left him I said, "Wiley you only have about twenty minutes before you have to run the trials of the 110 High Hurdles. The team needs you to qualify for the finals."

He quietly said, "Okay."

And he did it.

About an hour later, after he qualified for the finals in the hurdles, I asked one of our athletes to check on Wiley and see if he was okay while I prepared for the start of the 10000m. I moved away from the crowd to a spot along the backstretch so that my distance runners could hear me as they passed. Just before the gun went off, I noticed Wiley walking toward me. He didn't say anything about the long jump or the hurdles, he simply asked, "Coach, is there any way I can help?"

"Actually, yes. I was just looking for someone to help me write down times for Ferrier. Our two other runners are going to be toward the front. Ferrier is running a different plan. He is running a specific time. I don't care what place he is in, I just want him to be on pace. If he races the plan, and if some of the other team's runners go out too fast, he has a good chance to score for the team. I can't watch the front runners and Ferrier too.

As the race got under way, I recorded the times for the first runners. As Bret Ferrier would approach the lap mark, Wiley would shout out his time just before Bret got to me so that I could yell out instructions to Bret. Bret fell further and further behind.

Wiley began to worry. "Coach, should I tell him to go faster?"

"No, no… Not yet… Just have him run his pace. Remember, 'plan your race…'"

"Yeah, yeah, I know, '…and race your plan.'"

Some runners had scratched, leaving only ten runners in the 10K. Now, Bret only had to beat two other runners in order to score.

The first nine started fast, moving quite a ways ahead of Bret. At the mile mark, one started to fall off pace. Bret caught him and passed him. Bret was now in ninth place. He only needed to pass one other runner in order to score for our team. At the halfway mark, the lead runners were more than 100 meters ahead.

Wiley continued to give me Bret Ferrier's lap splits.

"Coach, he was within a tenth of a second of his target pace on that one!"

"Coach he was within two tenths on that lap!"

"Coach, that last lap was right on! He is doing exactly what you want him to do."

Wiley's excitement was contagious. Others teammates gathered around. Soon about half of our athletes surrounded us. I told them to be careful not to cheer too much for Ferrier until Wiley had told me his lap split, and I could offer him some coaching.

As the race proceeded, Ferrier continued to run well. He began to close the gap on the other athletes. Because of Wiley's help, Bret knew exactly what he was doing. With about one mile to go, he was in eighth place. Time to forget about lap times.

I unleashed him. Passing three more runners over the last lap, Ferrier placed fifth right behind our other two runners who took third and fourth in the race. As a team, they totaled fifteen points in that race, three more points than I had anticipated.

One of our long jumpers also came through for us, taking eighth in his event. After those two events and the conclusion of the first day of the conference meet we were only down by four points making up half of the eight points we lost in Wiley's long jump.

At the end of our team meeting, I did as I always do; I asked if anyone had anything to say. Wiley raised his hand and got up in front of the team. He apologized to the team for not doing what he felt he should have done in the long jump.

"I will do everything I possibly can to make up the points that I lost in the long jump. I know we are going to win, though, because I know that the points I can't make up, you will all be able to make up."

The next day he scored all the points we had planned for him to score by taking second place in the 110 high hurdles and fifth in the high jump. We were still down four points, though. As his triple jump event started, I left to watch some of the other events, because I felt that we would get more points over there than in the triple jump.

With two events left in the meet, I tried to calculate our team points won thus far in the meet and see where we stood. I was a bit worried.

Suddenly, Wiley came running toward me screaming, "Coach, I did it, I did it!"

"You scored points in the triple jump?"

"No… I *won* it!"

Wiley went into that event with a best mark five feet under the top competitor in the event and improved his seasonal best jump by more than five feet, winning the triple jump by six inches.

He more than made up for his lost points of the day before. In the process, he achieved a new personal record. We won the Big Sky Conference Championship by over twenty points.

By the end of his junior year, Wiley qualified for the NCAA Championships in the high hurdles. While he did not make the finals, he did achieve a new personal best, setting a new school record in the event.

As it turned out, Wiley King was the most talented athlete I ever worked with at Weber State. Over the course of his career, he set outdoor school records in the high hurdles, the long jump and in the 100m dash. We red-shirted him one year so that he could finish up with track after football and not be pulled two directions between spring football and the outdoor track season.

During his red-shirt year, Wiley approached me and asked what he could do to be an All-American. He thought I would be talking about the high hurdles, but I said, "I think the best shot you have at being an All-American is in the heptathlon."

"The what? The heptathlon?" he asked, somewhat confused.

"Well, yes. You already have four outstanding events – high jump, long jump, hurdles, and sprints. All you have to do is learn to pole vault, throw the shot put, and I'll get you into good enough shape to run the distance event."

"So, all I have to do is learn to pole vault and throw the shot? That's kind of a lot, don't you think?"

I said, "It will be a lot of work, but it is your best chance at becoming an All-American."

He took me up on it. During his red-shirt year, he learned the fundamentals of the pole vault, but it still wasn't a good enough mark to really help him in the heptathlon – not if he wanted to be right up at the top. He continued to work hard. He improved until he could vault near 14'. He also worked on his shot put. For his body size, he did very well, throwing close to 45'. We worked on the 1,000 meter run and he got to where he could sustain a 4:48 mile pace.

During his senior year, he continued to do an outstanding job. He became the Big Sky Conference All-time Career Top Scorer. He qualified for the NCAA National Meet in the Heptathlon entering the meet with the eighth top mark. [An athlete must finish in the top eight to be an All-American.]

On the first day of the heptathlon, all of his marks were just off from his qualifying standards. It looked doubtful that he would complete the second day of events as an All-American. After the first day, we figured out points, and Wiley asked, "Coach, what will I need to do to be an All-American?"

"Well…" I paused, looking over the marks and points to determine what Wiley would have to do. "You will need to run close to your all-time best in the hurdles – which I know you can do. Then you will have to set personal best marks in both the pole vault and the thousand meters. To make up for your point deficit, it will take at least as many total points as your personal best. Your first-day marks were not your best, so you are down about 100 points. You have to beat your other events by about 250 points in order to get that All-America certificate."

I told him he could do it – and he did.

He accomplished his goal in the hurdles, running very close to his personal best. In the pole vault, he exceeded his personal best of 13'11" three times. He cleared 14'3" 14'7" and then 14'11". He earned an additional 100 points. This was a terrific personal best!

After six events, he went into the 1000m race with sixth, seventh, eighth, and ninth places within fifteen points of each other.

"What do I need to do in the thousand?" he asked me.

"You need to have a twelve-second personal record. Instead of running 4:48 mile pace, you will have to run 4:36 pace."

This was a difficult challenge, especially given the adversity and disappointment that he experienced the first day; nevertheless, he was determined to give it everything he possibly could.

Wiley finished that race with breaking his personal record by *thirteen*-seconds. (He was unable to walk, even with assistance, for fifteen minutes!)

He placed sixth in the NCAA National Indoor Meet and achieved his goal of being an All-American.

The sixth place that he took was outstanding. The real thrill for me, however, was to watch how he fought his way back after a disappointing first day. Some of the other athletes who had experienced disappointment on the first day of competition allowed that mentality to carry over into the second day and it brought them down. Wiley used the adverse circumstances of a tough first day to enhance his efforts on the second. He fought back hard the next day with personal records in each event (including three in the pole vault alone) and won his All-America certificate.

Every time Wiley faced adversity during his athletic career, he always found a way to dig deep into his soul and get back on track with an outstanding performance. He always maintained the physical, mental, and emotional presence of a champion – no matter how he felt.

He finished his career with an All-Time Outdoor Big Sky Conference record – *108 points!*

11

John Webb

Wrestling with Failure

Failure is the line of least persistence.
> ~ *Zig Ziglar quoting Abraham Lincoln*

When your trials seem great and your rewards seem few,
remember the mighty oak was once a nut like you.
> ~ *Bullwinkle*

Be like a postage stamp – stick to one thing until you
get there.
> ~ *Josh Billings*

Good, better and best never let me rest, until my good is my
better and my better is my best.
> ~*Tim Dunkin or St. Jerome*

I coached wrestling for five years at Weber State. When I first took
over the program, Weber was at the bottom of the conference – so
naturally I decided to mount a challenge for the championship!

The first year we had good wrestlers at the two lower weight classes,
so we started out fairly well. We struggled however, because we
were lacking in the 134-pound weight class. Sometimes we didn't
even have a body to fill the slot.

I went to Green River, Wyoming, during the Christmas holidays to officiate a high school wresting meet. One of their coaches told me that a young man who had wrestled his freshman year at the University of Wyoming had just returned from a two-year religious commitment and had decided not to go back to Wyoming. Instead, he was thinking of attending Ricks Junior College.

He wrestled at 118 pounds before he left for his two-year commitment. He had grown enough in those two years that he might be big enough to wrestle at 134 – but his weight gain wasn't all muscle!

I was in my motel room between wrestling sessions. There was a knock on my door, and here was this little redheaded, almost orange-haired, young man. He introduced himself as John Webb and said he was a wrestler. He was long and thin; built more like a distance runner than a wrestler.

I offered him half of my ham and cheese sandwich. That's how I recruited John Webb!

John came to our wrestling program in January of that year. It did not take long to discover that he did not have the physical traits necessary to be a collegiate wrestler. His reaction time was poor. He was too slow. He was comparatively weak. He did not have the overall strength to compete against athletes who might weigh up to 150 pounds and would drop enough weight to wrestle at 134.

One thing John did have, however, was determination – and he filled our need to have a body in the 134 weight class.

It was in his heart to be a successful wrestler. He accepted the fact that he did not have the fundamental physical characteristics of an outstanding collegiate wrestler, so he spent many hours developing strategies that would turn his disadvantages into advantages. He did not have the speed necessary to be good offensive wrestler; therefore, he had to become an outstanding defensive wrestler.

Because he was slow on his feet, he knew his opponents would likely be able to get into his legs and take him down. He focused on developing strategies to turn the tables on his opponents by shifting their offensive moves into defensive takedowns.

John developed a cross-face move that pushed his opponent backward, so he could then try to turn it into a cross-face cradle. It worked occasionally, but it was not enough. Eventually, he came up with a complete series of moves from the cross-face.

If his opponent turned one way, John would use one type of a cross-face move. If a person turned another way, he would put him into a cross-face cradle. If a person turned yet another way, he would respond with a step-over. If the person moved upward, John would apply a whip-over. He developed a complete series.

This did not happen overnight. It took over a thousand repetitions over a period of two years to perfect this series of moves.

During his first year at Weber State, he ended up the season with three wins and eighteen losses. Predictably, he had not demonstrated the physical abilities required for a collegiate wrestler. But, remember, the reason he was there was to fill in the 134 weight class spot and *maybe* get some wins for us.

At the end of that year, I asked him if he wanted to continue to wrestle, or if I should recruit someone else.

He said, "No, Coach. I will win consistently for the team before we're through."

I had my doubts, but he did have two things he going for him: heart and determination. He continued to work out longer and harder than anyone else. He continued to work on his series and his method. During his next year, his junior year, he ended up with about seventeen wins, fifteen losses. Surprisingly, he took third place in the conference meet.

In the second half of his junior year, John had an opportunity to wrestle a Division Two national champion from San Francisco State. The wrestler would take John down very easily; so easily in fact, that he would let John back up so he could take him down again and rack up more points. He'd get two for a take-down, and John would get one point for an escape. They were still in the first period, with the score at eight to three, when the young man got a nosebleed. A time out was called.

John came over to me with a big smile on his face, "I've got him where I want him. I'll win for sure, Coach."

I said, "*You* have *him* where *you* want *him*? John, he's taking you down at will!"

He said, "Oh, no. He's getting tired. Didn't you notice? The last time I almost was able to get my cross-face in. He's slowing down! The next time he tries to take me down, I'll get one of my cross-face moves in!"

He really believed it, too.

The San Francisco State wrestler had his choice of position to start the second round. He took the 'up' position. As soon as the referee started the round, he pushed John away and started to shoot another takedown on John. This time John stopped him with his cross-face and put him on his back with a whip-over.

"Oh boy, he might have a chance to pin him!"

As soon as John got his three points for having him on his back, he let him off of his back. Then he put him on his back again with a cross-face cradle. In about fifteen seconds, John scored one point for an escape, two points for a takedown, three points for a near fall, and three points for another near fall taking the lead with a twelve to eight score.

The last round started. It was John's turn to be on top. John decided that he wanted to win further. Instead of trying to turn him and keep him down, John let him up!

The guy looked at John and must have thought, "You idiot! Now I can win this match!"

So he shot at John for a takedown again. John stopped him with his cross-face cradle, and put him on his back once again. After trailing 3 to 8 at the end of the first round, John ended up winning 21 to 9 with a superior decision (winning by more than ten points) against a Division II National Champion.

The hundreds of extra hours John spent in the wrestling room working on his cross-face series paid off. He would be a very successful wrestler if he continued to *identify the strong points of his opponent's and turn them to his benefit.*

By the time his senior year started, John had become an outstanding and confident wrestler. He was still tall and thin for his weight class. He had built his strength up so it was average. His reaction was still slow. However he was brilliant at thinking on his feet and anticipating the moves of his opponent. Strategic thinking was his gift. John went into the conference meet with a 25/4 win/loss record.

One of his losses was to another talented redhead from Idaho State – a wrestler John had also beaten in a different match. They were aggressive, skilled, and smart. They had stacked up over twenty wins each for the season. They were wrestling for the Big Sky Conference Championship. The winner would go to the NCAA Championships. The loser would stay home.

John told me when I recruited him three years earlier that his goal was to go to the NCAA Championship Meet. I didn't mention that earlier because it would have sounded ridiculous. During his sophomore year he could not even beat poor to average local wrestlers.

Now, in his senior year, competing in the NCAA meet was clearly possible.

The Big Sky Conference 134 pound match was one of the best wrestling matches I've ever seen. Both came out aggressively. One would attack. The other would counter. Then the other would attack and the first would counter. They just kept at it; aggressively seeking the win. The referee told me afterward that he had never been so physically tired after a match; there was so much action.

With fifteen seconds to go, this outstanding match was tied. John wasn't willing to let it go into overtime. He wanted to win it in the last fifteen seconds. As he shot in to take his opponent down, his back leg slipped, and he fell to his side. Before he could recover his balance, the Idaho State wrestler quickly maneuvered behind him and got two points for a takedown.

John immediately escaped, earning one point, putting him one point behind. He shot in again, but the opponent countered. John kept going after him. He got the takedown a split second after the buzzer sounded.

It was a legitimate call. He did not win. His dream was shattered.

As he came off the mat, he burst into tears. I got him away from the crowd as fast as I could. We stood together at edge of the bleachers. He was leaning on my shoulder sobbing, "I lost. I lost. I'll never go to a national meet."

For some reason, I don't know why, I whispered, "John, you will go. You will get to your national meet. I don't know how you will do it, but you will go."

The next Monday, we got a call from Idaho State saying that the young man from Idaho State was injured in a freak accident and would be unable to go to the NCAA meet. They wanted to know if John would go. We jumped at the opportunity.

We had to get it approved through the NCAA Rules Committee. We just thought it would be a formality, and that somehow I had been right when I told John that he would get to fulfill his dream of going to go to the National Championships.

We checked with the NCAA. 134 was the best weight in the conference that year, but the NCAA said that they did not have a policy that would permit the substitution. The person who earned the right to go had to go. If he was unable to go, we had to leave the spot open. We petitioned and attempted to get it through. We were not successful. It was decided that John would not get to go. The spot must remain open and The Big Sky would not be represented at the NCAA meet in our strongest weight class. Neither of these two outstanding young men would represent us at the NCAA championships.

John's collegiate career was over.

For years, it bothered me that I had told him he would somehow get to go, when I knew the odds for that happening were nearly insurmountable. At the moment, it felt right in telling him that he would, but it had not worked out. What was I thinking?

John wanted to be a high school teacher and coach. He majored in Secondary Education and, after graduation, was hired as the head coach at Weber High School – starting right out as the head wrestling coach at a major high school.

In two years, John transformed Weber High School's relatively poor wrestling team into a state contender. By the end of the second year, they were fighting for the state championship.

During those two years, about once a week, I would get a call at 9:30 at night. My wife would say (as if she didn't know), "Who's that?"

I would mouth the words, "John Webb."

She would sigh and say, "I am going to bed." She knew it would be at least a two-hour conversation about coaching and coaching techniques.

John was just as persistent in his coaching as he was in his participation and he knew that coaches need coaching. As the time went on, he would seek knowledge and technique from every source he could find. He would talk to other collegiate coaches as well as to me. He sought out mentors at every level. His level of knowledge, and his ability to convey it to his athletes, grew exponentially.

By the end of his third year, he had three state champion wrestlers. His team took second in the state in a very close battle with the predominate Brighton High School.

At that time I decided it was time for me to concentrate on just one sport. I got out of wrestling to focus on track & field. That put Weber State in need of a wrestling coach. Though John was relatively inexperienced for a collegiate coach, I felt he would be a good candidate for the job. I suggested that he apply for it.

It came down to two finalists for the job: high school coach John Webb and a University of Utah assistant coach who had also been a NCAA champion. They were both interviewed.

After the interview, the athletic director told me what they decided. The college assistant coach had more experience. He demonstrated a little more knowledge. He seemed better qualified. It sounded like John was coming in second again. In the next sentence, however, the athletic director revealed, "But I chose Webb. There is just something about him. I know he's going to be successful."

Sometimes you meet an athlete, an applicant, an employee who is obviously not the best qualified for the job – but then...

I replied, "You could not have said it better. John Webb will find a way to win."

A few minutes later, my office phone rang. It was John. "Coach, you were right all along."

Perplexed, I asked, "I was right about what?"

"I'm going to go to the NCAA Wrestling Championships. I'll get one of my athletes there. That means I will get there after all – just like you said!"

John showed the same persistence and dedication as a coach that he had as a wrestler. He spent as many hours as necessary trying to help every wrestler develop championship level technique. It was incredible how much his athletes improved in the time he had with them. They were not only well-conditioned, but the technique level they developed under John's guidance was incredible.

In just two years, John had developed his first NCAA All-American. Perseverance, hard work, grit, dedication, and determination create amazing possibilities even when the odds are stacked against you. That is what Coach John Webb is all about.

In fact, Coach Webb developed *five* All-Americans in the four years he coached at Weber State before we had to drop the program because of Title IX. All of his recruits were local high school athletes. His program elevated more Utah wrestlers to the status of All-American than any other university in the state.

12

A Beg-On...

...Never Accepts "No"

Do not let what you cannot do interfere with what you
can do.
   ~ *John Wooden*

Success depends more upon attitude than upon aptitude.
   ~ *William James*

For they conquer who believe they can.
   ~ *Virgil*

A "walk-on" is someone you would really like to be on your team
but, because the athlete's ability and achievements don't measure
up to some of the other recruited athletes, scholarship money
isn't available.

Of course, someone who might be a "walk-on" at a larger school
– one that might be vying for a national championship – may very
well be a scholarship athlete at a smaller school.

Such it was at "little ol' Webber State." If we didn't have scholarship
money for an athlete (which happened more often than we wished),
but we thought he had potential to help the team later in his college
career, we would invite him to "walk-on" as a freshman.

When I first got the coaching job at Weber State, I determined to never turn down a local athlete who expressed an interest in competing on the cross country or track & field teams. As long as they were motivated, I would try to provide these athletes with an opportunity to prove themselves.

Some who came to me asking for a chance to compete did not even qualify as "walk-ons." I call them "beg-ons." These were usually students I knew little about or just didn't think had the ability to make the team. Most of them would show up the first day of school, not having done any conditioning over the summer, and plead, "Coach, I want to be on the track team."

I would ask them a few questions and, after finding out their lack of conditioning and/or apparent ability, I would try to discourage them. They would then have to convince me that they deserved a shot at making the team. They would also have to demonstrate that they could and would do everything I required of my scholarship athletes.

They almost literally had to beg their way onto the team, hence the term, "beg-ons."

They would typically get a thirty-day trial period after which we would meet again to determine whether or not they wanted to continue. Usually they had not yet convinced me that they *deserved* a spot on the team; still, they did have a chance to explain how much they *wanted* to be on the team.

These "beg-ons" had often been told, "You aren't good enough." "You can't do it." "You'll never make it." High school coaches had said, "Enjoy your high school running career, because you're not good enough to compete in college."

These determined beg-ons were highly motivated to prove wrong those who had told them they couldn't do it. Many of these young athletes, who continued to improve and finally made the team, became some of my favorite athletes because of their personality, character, intelligence and dogged determination. There have been many over the years – at least one or two on every conference team.

Principle among their shared characteristics was their ability and *willingness* to work hard. Despite a lack of natural ability, or perhaps because of it, these men tended to work harder and longer, than the other more naturally gifted members of the team. They were goal-driven. They were vision focused. They were clear about their athletic goals and aspirations and determined to do whatever it took to achieve them.

They were eager, coachable, and intelligent. They paid close attention to the reasoning and methodology behind our training regimen. Though they hadn't yet achieved the level of success of most of their more talented teammates, they were confident and success-oriented. They stayed on track, believing that the quantity and quality of their hard work would yield a greater outcome than natural talent alone.

These determined athletes had supreme faith in themselves and faith in a Supreme Being who cared for them in a very personal way, and would support them in their worthy endeavor of achieving their personal best.

Over the years, I have had many, many great and successful begons. The following three chapters are the stories of three of them.

13

Jason Schoenfeld

Beg-On Extraordinaire

Win if you can; lose if you must; but *never quit!*
  ~ *Cameron Trammell*

Never give up! Failure and rejection are only the first steps
to succeeding.
  ~ *Jim Valvano*

The hardest skill to acquire in this sport is the one where you
compete all out, give it all you have, and you are still getting
beat no matter what you do. When you have the killer instinct
to fight through that, it is very special.
  ~ *Eddie Reese*

Champions keep playing until they get it right.
  ~ *Billie Jean King*

Jason Schoenfeld was perhaps the champion "beg-on" of all time.
He hailed from a local Utah high school. Over his three-year high
school career, he had clocked a 4:48 mile and ran about 10:10 in
the two-mile. I did not recruit Jason. I did not even ask him to come
out for the team as a "walk-on." On the first day of practice, he
approached me and said, "Coach, I want to be on your track and
cross country teams."

I did tell him, politely, that he was welcome to try out. I also told him it was highly unlikely that he would make the team. I always hated to do this, but it is a core trait with me to be honest. I've never seen a Shetland Pony win the Kentucky Derby – though it sure would make my heart proud to see one try!

With a big smile, Jason asked what time practice started. He assured me that he would be at every workout – on time.

If it hadn't been for the supportive team spirit of my athletes, Jason would have been a laughingstock – he really was that bad. On distance runs, the team would have been back for at least twenty minutes; when someone would finally ask, "Where's Jason?" Another would reply, "Oh, he's not back yet, wait another fifteen minutes. He'll show up." And he would.

On ten-mile runs, Jason was typically between two or three minutes *per mile* behind the other members of the team. As the season progressed, Jason lessened the gap to a minute to a minute and a half per mile. Despite the fact that he was not able to keep up with the group, he showed up for practice every day and worked hard. He slowly chipped away at the substantial time gap that separated him from the other runners.

We red-shirted Jason his freshman year. He simply wasn't good enough to compete. Because he was slower than the others, he ran alone most of the time; therefore, he didn't get a lot of attention or direct encouragement from the other athletes or the coaches. He was quiet, listened intently, and faithfully executed his instructions just as he was told.

He improved quite a bit but was far from being a quality runner. At the end of his freshman year, I figured he'd had enough. I did not expect him to try out the next year. In fact, he approached me at the end of that year to tell me that he had decided to fulfill a religious commitment and would be gone for the next two years. I admit to a feeling of relief. Then he added, "I'll be back, I want to come back."

I just smiled. I assumed that after two years away, he would realize that he was not cut out for college track. I was wrong.

He left in June, immediately after his freshman year, and he returned two years later in June. He began to train with some of the athletes who were around over the summer. By the end of August, he only trailed the team by thirty seconds a mile on a ten mile run.

He came up to me just before the start of the next season and said, "Coach, I don't think I am quite ready to run for Weber State."

Relieved, I thought, "Good. I'm glad you have come to your senses. You need to get on with your life." But I didn't say it.

His next comment caught me by surprise, "I can't quite run with Weber State *yet,* so I think I will join the military for a couple of years. That doesn't count against my eligibility, so I will be back."

Off he went to serve his country.

Two years later, Jason showed up again. He had used his time in the service well. He had trained every day by himself putting in over sixty miles a week, improving his ability and endurance immensely.

He returned to school once again wanting to participate in track and cross country. At this point, Jason had been out of high school for five years – one year as a red-shirt freshman, two years serving his church, and another two years serving his country. It was, therefore, Jason's *sixth* year out of high school that he started his freshman year of NCAA eligibility at Weber State. Though he continued to improve that year, he still did not make the traveling squad in the cross country, indoor, or outdoor track.

At the beginning of his sophomore year (now his seventh year out of High School), Jason finally demonstrated his ability to stay with the team on a ten-mile distance run. In the harder, faster interval workouts, however, he still lagged far behind.

He failed again to make the cross country traveling team.

Though he was still not good enough to be one of our top runners, he was definitely improving; so I gave him a chance to compete in one or two of our home indoor track meets that season.

We had twenty five spaces available on our traveling squad for the Big Sky Conference Meet that season. Twenty three athletes had achieved conference qualifying marks, but we were allowed two wild-card spots for athletes who had not made the qualifying standard.

Looking over the roster to determine who should go in the wild-card positions, I considered two field athletes. Then, because of Jason's tenacity over the past several years and his recent improvement I tossed his name into the mix. This opportunity could provide Jason with some well-deserved personal satisfaction. Besides, it just seemed the right thing to do.

I informed my assistant coach, Dan Walker, that I had given one wild-card slot to Jason Schoenfeld and would leave it up to him to decide which of his two field-event athletes would fill the other slot.

Dan looked at me in shock, "Why? Why would you take Jason Schoenfeld? He will not score a single point in the conference meet."

His comment incited my ire, so I called upon one of my brilliant classic responses. "Wanna bet?"

"Yeah, I'll bet on this," he shot back.

"It might not be at this meet, but he will place in a conference meet. Anyone who wants something that badly and works that hard will find a way to accomplish it," I said.

We took Jason to the meet that year and he set a personal best record which, given his previous record, wasn't saying a lot. But at least he did not place last! He placed thirteenth among the fifteen athletes in his event – a definite improvement, but still a long way from showing that he deserved a permanent spot on our traveling team.

As luck would have it, the outdoor conference meet that year was to be held at Weber State. Jason began to compete more often during the outdoor season. It became apparent that the longer the race, the better for Jason because he wouldn't have to run quite as close to his top speed. By the time the conference meet arrived, there was an outside chance that Jason could place in the 10000m race (at the time the 10K did not have a qualifying standard) and thereby score points for Weber.

We had an outstanding team that year, so once again I had to pick who would round off the squad as our wild card athletes. Once more the choice came down to three. I chose Jason over a Javelin thrower who had the ninth best throw in the Big Sky Conference.

Now, I felt like the "beg-on." I had to convince my assistant coach for the second time that Jason deserved the wild-card spot – even over a perhaps more accomplished athlete. He could compete in the 5K as well as the 10K. Because these distance events would be held at our home track and at altitude, he had an outside chance of placing in one of them.

Coach Walker reluctantly agreed.

When we received the entries for the 10K, I was surprised to see that there were only ten entrants. Perhaps because the event was to be contested at altitude, many of the coaches had decided to hold athletes out of the 10K and run them in the 5K instead. After seven years of dedicated work, Jason might have a chance to finally place in a conference meet. I examined the list. Jason *might* be able to capture eighth place (the last place that would score points in the conference meet). It would be great for his morale and confidence.

It was an exceptionally warm day. As the race started, Jason had to be careful not to go out too quickly and to run within his ability. This is where his intelligence came into play. He realized that he simply had to race his plan and stay diligently on pace.

He wasn't embarrassed to spend the entirety of the first mile in last place, running within his capabilities. The altitude and the heat took its toll on some of the other athletes. By the three-mile mark, Jason had moved into *seventh* position, the distance widening between him and the three runners behind him as they continued to drop off their paces.

At this point, it seemed obvious that Jason was going to score at least two points for his team. Everyone could see the drive and determination on his face. He looked strong. Sixth and fifth place were only about thirty meters ahead. By the fifth mile, Jason caught and passed both of these runners. With a mile left in the race, fourth place was actually within reach – only fifty meters ahead.

Given that the race was held at Weber, and that Jason was a local athlete, many of the fans knew him and his history. Jason quickly became the crowd favorite – receiving more attention than our two 10K front-runners.

Starting the bell-lap, Jason pulled up behind the fourth runner. He had 300 meters to go. Since he lacked natural leg speed we encouraged him to make a bid for fourth place at that point rather than wait and try to beat his competitor over the final fifty meters.

As Jason went by, the athlete he passed deflated realizing he had lost his fourth place position. Jason finished fourth in the race, achieving another personal best and earning *five* points for his team.

As soon as the race was over, I went over to my assistant coach and put out my hand. Dan shook it.

"I don't want you to shake my hand." I said, "I want you to pay up!"

He reached into his pocket and handed over the traditional bet – a shiny nickel.

"This kid has two years left, and he will be a conference champion before his time is done," I declared confidently.

Coach Walker looked me up and down. "Is that another bet?"

"Yes. Are you willing to risk another nickel?"

Even though there were many other athletes running the 5K fresh the next day, Jason was able to take sixth place. The points he earned for us in that meet were the equivalent of a second place finish.

Placing in this meet and earning significant points for his team jump-started Jason's career. He began to run even better races and contribute more and more points to his team scores.

Keep in mind that in the seven years Jason had been out of high school, he had only made two road trips with the team. Also keep in mind that he was a hard worker and determined to succeed. After placing in the Big Sky meet, he increased his mileage to over eighty quality miles a week.

Jason's junior year was a turning point. He began to excel during our fall cross country season and earned a spot among our top competitors. He placed well in cross country and even higher in indoor track.

After the indoor season I approached him with an idea, "Jason, you have earned the right to go out to Palo Alto, California and run the 10k at the Stanford meet."

He was delighted! He understood the significance of the Stanford meet. It was a prestigious, traditional event where he would be competing with some of the best NCAA runners in the nation. In addition, our school paid for these athletes to fly to California instead of taking a two-day bus trip to the competition. Flying with the team was another first for Jason.

Our goal was for him run fast enough to qualify for the NCAA National Meet. I predicted that he would run 6.2 miles with a per mile pace average ten seconds faster than his high school personal best for one mile. That is what it would take to qualify for the national meet. I believed he could and would – and he did!

He stayed on pace, and closed his last 400 meters in 61 seconds. This was an unbelievable speed for him at that time. He qualified for the NCAA National Meet at Stanford. Two weeks later he won the Big Sky Conference Title in the 10K meters. Jason also became NCAA All-American in the 10K.

One more shiny nickel plopped into my bank!

Jason continued to stay on track with his program of improvement during his senior year. He achieved All-American honors in cross country. After many more successes over the course of his indoor and outdoor track seasons, he competed in the NCAA Outdoor Championship Meet and earned his third All-American certificate. All of this happened near the end of his collegiate career, after he had been out of high school for *nine* years.

How could someone with apparently so little natural talent accomplish such honors? Faith and belief in oneself combined with his hard work and dedication *does* pay off. Whenever I see Jason, we reminisce about what a great runner he became because of his dedication and persistence; and how glad I am that he "begged-on" and became part of Weber State's running legacy.

14

Clark Roberts

Built like a Brick – Runs like a Champ

Whether you think you can, or think you can't, you are right.
~ Henry Ford

The Four D's: Discipline, Desire, Determination
and Dedication.
~ Billy Casper

The oldest, shortest words, "yes" and "no," are those which
require the most thought.
~ Pythagoras

Clark Roberts' father was an outstanding history professor at Weber
State. Whenever and wherever our paths crossed, he would corner
me and brag on about how great a runner his son was.

His father assumed that because his son was one of the best runners
on his track team that he was an outstanding track athlete. The
problem was that his high school had a poorly developed track
program – so anyone who did anything would look quite good.

Clark's record proved, however, that he was not another Roger
Bannister. His high school time for the mile was just under 5:00 and

his two-mile time was about 10:40. He was a below average high school distance runner.

Actually, what he was best at was wrestling. He was built like a wrestler: short and stocky, with the powerful legs of a linebacker. He had placed in the Utah State Wrestling Championships in the 132 pound class. So, when Clark showed up at my door on the first day of school, I naturally directed him to see the wrestling coach.

He responded flatly, "I don't want to be a wrestler. I want to be a runner."

He was determined to run. Well, since he was a local athlete, and pretty good at begging, I allowed him to come out for the cross country team. It didn't take me long to realize that his dad was, inadvertently, right. He was, or could become, a strong runner. He also had great flexibility, probably developed during his wrestling career. I soon pegged him as a steeplechaser.

He worked hard and followed carefully our coaching team's guidance. He enjoyed some success as a freshman, placing sixth in the steeplechase at the conference meet. At the end of that year, Clark decided to serve a religious mission for his church.

He returned two years later and came out for the team once again. He made significant improvement, holding his own with my nine-minute steeplechasers during workouts. The trouble was, when it came time for the race, Clark would stay on pace for about five laps, then fall apart and drop off pace by twenty to thirty seconds. He did this in three consecutive races.

"Coach, I am doing the same workouts as everyone else," he said, "but I'm not holding up. I talk to my teammates about how they feel during a race. They say that it hurts some but they're okay. Coach, my legs get so heavy, I can hardly handle the water jump. I just don't know what to do."

I felt like attributing his fatigue to the fact that he had oak tree stumps instead of legs; but I thought better of it. Mocking isn't very motivational. Instead I told him to let me think about it and I'd find a solution.

The steeplechase barriers are essentially immovable hurdles. As Brad Barton says, "In the hurdles you hit a hurdle and it goes down. In the steeplechase you hit a hurdle and *you* go down!"

The common way to negotiate the water barrier is for the athlete to push off from the top of the barrier, clearing as much of the twelve foot water pit as they can, landing as far out in in the shallow end as possible so as not to reduce their speed.

When Clark told me how fatigued he felt during the race, I wondered what would happen if, instead of placing his foot on the top of the water barrier and lifting the entirety of his body weight in order to push off and clear the water on the other side, we would have him simply hurdle this barrier as he did the others. He would land sooner and deeper in the water, but the change in technique might help preserve his energy and might allow him to apply his leg strength to come out of the water.

No one did that then, but there are some that do it now. Innovation is sometimes the name of the game.

Two weeks later we had another meet. He hurdled all of his water jumps. This rare technique excited onlookers as they crowded around the water pit. After the fifth lap and the point where Clark had been falling off the pace, he was still right with his teammates. He glanced over at me with a grin and gave me a "thumbs up." Then, instead of dropping back as he had in the past, he surged ahead, running each of the last two laps faster than any of the earlier laps. In that single race, he improved his time by twenty-six seconds!

It was possibly the most significant one-time improvement I ever saw in a steeplechase athlete. He was extremely excited. It changed his entire outlook.

At the conference meet that spring, Weber took three of the top four spots in the steeplechase. Clark came in fourth behind two of our other outstanding athletes. One of them went on to become a National Champion. The other became an All-American in the steeplechase. Clark beat all but one of the steeplechasers from the other schools.

The next fall, during the cross country season, we felt our team could achieve the national "Sweet Sixteen." In order to achieve that rank, Clark had to run as a strong fifth man – or better.

Through the first three meets, Clark was running in sixth or seventh position on the team – and not racing at the level his workouts indicated he could. I wondered why. When I talked with him about it, it became evident that his problem was in his head, not in his legs. He simply didn't believe he had what it took to consistently run at the level he had demonstrated in the steeplechase during the conference meet the previous spring. I told him he had to stop pigeon-holing himself as a seventh man and get out and run with our top runners. He wasn't convinced.

I decided the best way to show him how good he was and how much he had improved was to run him in a race where there were no other Weber State runners. Instead of having him run in the last scheduled meet with the rest of the team, I took Clark to Pocatello, Idaho to run alone in a meet where he did not know the abilities of any of the top runners in the field.

During the two-hour drive to the meet, I asked him a critical question: "Clark, do you think I would ask you to do something you are not capable of doing?"

"No," he responded.

"Well, good. Now, today I want you to just go out and run with the leaders."

"I'll try coach."

"No. Don't try, DO!" (Yoda learned that from me!)

He looked at me and grinned, "Okay, okay, yes... *I will.*"

When the race started Clark went right to the front of the pack and ran with the leaders for four and a half miles. He then took the lead and won by ten seconds, breaking his own personal record by *fifty* seconds.

Talk about exceeding one's personal best! A fifty-second difference in a five mile race? That's a ten seconds per mile improvement!

During our debriefing, I pointed out that he had beaten two runners that our fourth man had never beaten. He replied, "Ya know coach, I never really thought of myself as a cross country runner."

I smiled, "Do you now?"

"Yep! I do now!"

Our team took eleventh in the NCAA meet that year. One of the main reasons we finished as high as we did was because Clark became a very strong *third* man. His intelligence, tenacity, constant desire to stay on track and move his *attitude* outside its comfort zone, propelled Clark from a questionable "beg-on" freshman to a three time All-Conference performer.[12]

---

12   Clark Roberts also achieved the remarkable status of a four-time All-Conference Academic Award winner.

15

Ken Richardson

One's Attitude Depends on One's Attitude

Your attitude is either a key or a lock.
> ~ *[unknown]*

The most difficult thing is the decision to act – the rest is merely tenacity.
> ~ *Amelia Earhart*

A great distance runner can't run any further or faster than anyone else, but he does anyway.
> ~ *Brad Barton*

One of the most important traits of a potentially successful "beg-on" is how quickly the athlete can, and is inclined to, improve. "Beg-ons" come in all different shapes and sizes and levels of ability. It isn't just their ability to improve that matters, it is the willingness, the desire, the natural inclination to improve. This is what I look for in an athlete, even more important than their natural talent and record of achievement.

Attitude is to an athlete what tracks are to a train.

The first day of school, Ken Richardson came to the track and asked if he could join the cross country team. I asked where he was from.

"Bingham High School."

"Oh! Bingham! Good! What position were you on the team last year?" I asked.

Bingham had one of the best distance programs in the state. I thought, perhaps, Ken was a decent runner, but someone I didn't know that much about. If he was from Bingham, he might be, or could become, an outstanding runner.

"Eighth..." Then he mumbled, "Sometimes."

Eighth was the highest place he had finished. In fact, he was not consistently placing even that high. He also revealed that he had never broken a five-minute mile in an official meet.

Ken was on a Presidential Scholarship. This indicated intelligence, one of my main criteria for accepting a "beg on." He was also a local athlete so, despite his mediocre record, I was willing to let him try out for the cross country team.

During the first few weeks of practice, I discovered that Ken was in a late growth spurt. He had grown about three inches over the last year and was still growing. That made a significant difference in what he could possibly accomplish as a distance runner.

As the fall went on and the indoor season approached, Ken improved significantly. I got a firmer grasp of his capabilities and potential. I decided to take him to our first indoor meet. I told him that he was to run a consistent, consecutive 72-second 400 pace for a two-mile race. That meant he had to go through the first mile in 4:48.

He looked at me in disbelief, "Coach, you want me to go through the first mile of a two mile in 4:48? My best mile time is 5:00!"

"Yes. That is exactly what I want from you. I want you to do it because I know you are capable of it."

"Okay, coach. I will do the first mile that way, but I can't promise what will happen after that."

"Ken, *I* can promise *you* what will happen after that – if you run our plan for your first mile."

"Really? What will happen?"

"You'll run the second mile just as fast."

"We'll see if I can."

"Well, you can if you will. It's up to you."

The gun went off, starting the two-mile race. Ken got a little excited and ran the first 400 in 69 seconds instead of our planned 72-second pace. He heard his split, recognized that he was fast, so he slowed to 72-second pace for the next three laps. His first mile split was 4:45 – a fifteen-second personal best at that distance, with still a mile left in the race.

He continued to run close to pace. With 600 meters to go, he got caught up in the dynamics of the race and began to pass his competition. He ran his last mile in 4:42 clocking a 9:27 two-mile time – more than a 60 second improvement over his best high-school time.

That day, Ken established three personal records – in one race. He set a personal best for the mile in the first mile of the race. He then broke that record with his second mile. His third personal best of the day was his overall time in the two-mile.

Usually a "beg-on" does not have that kind of success at such an early point in his career. Ken progressed from a "beg-on" to a "walk-on" in a single season. He still needed a lot of improvement, however, in order to be a scholarship athlete.

We decided that Ken's best event was the steeplechase. He did improve some during his freshman year – enough to warrant my taking him to the Junior National meet that year.

The excitement of that meet got to him in a negative way and he ran poorly, ending his freshman year on a low note. There was some disciplinary benefit in this. He had seen so much early success that this race gave him some much needed perspective. There was much more work to be done for him to achieve All American status.

During his next three years at Weber State, Ken continued to stay on track with his program of improvement. He became our cross country team's top runner, with the equivalent of an 8:54 two-mile and a 4:08 mile. He qualified for the NCAA Championship Meet twice in the steeplechase. These were outstanding marks for a guy who couldn't make his high school cross country team or even break a five-minute mile.

What stands out the most in his athletic career was that two-mile race his freshman year and his conference race his senior year.

Ken's faith in himself, his coach, and the program gave him the will to attempt, and the ability to accomplish, what seemed impossible a few short months earlier. His attitude and approach continued to help him improve throughout his career at Weber State.

His potential was never more evident than in the steeplechase in the Big Sky Conference meet his senior year. Ken was to compete against Swedish runner, Henrik Ahnstrom of Northern Arizona University. Ahnstrom had the fourth best time in the NCAA for that year.

The day before the race Ken came into my office and asked, "Coach, do you think I can beat Henrik"

Without hesitation I replied, "No, I don't *think* you can beat Henrik, I *know* you can beat Henrik. There is no way you'll let him beat you in your last conference meet at home – is there!"

With a determined look, he replied "No, there isn't!

As they lined up for the race the next day I knew Ken was going to push the race from the start. This was his last conference meet as a senior. He would use all the qualities he had developed over his last four years at Weber State. He had his plan. He was focused. He was determined to stay on track and race his plan no matter how good his opposition was.

By the end of the first mile Ken and Henrik were fifty yards ahead of the field. Ken pushed harder. Then it happened. Henrik broke! He began to fade, dropping further and further back until he was no longer even in the top three. Ken pushed on for another win.

What a great victory – especially for a "beg on!"

EPILOGUE

by Chick Hislop

> To bear up under loss, to fight the bitterness of defeat ... to go on ... to seek ever after the glory and dream, to look up with unquenchable faith ... that is what anyone can do, and so be great.
>
> ~ *Zane Grey*

Do you need a coach? I do. Everyone does. We always need a coach – or a mentor. Mentors need mentors. Coaches need coaches – all of our lives. It is a constant.

My dad often told me, "Don't re-invent the wheel every time you do something new. Others have done, or taught, what you are trying to do. Get their advice. They likely know a better way to accomplish what may be a new task to you."

The main job of a coach is to inspire and energize others to do their best – get better – establish a personal record – maybe do something that has never yet been done.

It is also to keep them focused on failure.

What? "Focus on failure?" Yes. Athletes need to always understand that failure is only a temporary change in direction to set them straight for the next level of success; that the willingness to fail – to crash and burn – then rise again – is a natural process required of the true champion.

149

Having said that, a coach cannot make people do something they are not capable of, but a good coach can and should enhance the attitude and improve the abilities physically, mentally – perhaps even spiritually – and put them in position to succeed.

Good coaches constantly find ways to improve the personal best of those they coach and prepare their charges to get in the habit of exceeding their personal best in business, at home, and in life – for the rest of their lives.

Great coaches also improve themselves in the process.

Most people believe that coaches must have "been there, done that." I admit to feeling inadequate at one point early in my career because I thought "been there done that" meant the coach had to have actually succeeded at the task; after all, how can you expect someone to do something that you've never done?

As the years passed, I learned that "been there done that" really means that good coaches have learned how to coach the task and are willing to share their knowledge and expertise with their charges – not prove they can personally do it – certainly not at the level they push their athletes to perform.

Great coaches break down skills and procedures and train in a way that makes success simple for the less experienced person to understand and reach for.

This is not natural. It takes special skill and focus to be willing and able to take apart athletic techniques; to strategize and train almost minuscule, incremental improvements measured in split seconds and fractions of inches.

Those to whom something has come naturally have not typically had to scientifically analyze what they are doing. That is why great athletes do not necessarily make the best coaches.

Often non-gifted athletes and others who had to work very hard to learn a skill have an advantage in teaching that skill to someone else. They have had to develop an intimate understanding of the intricacies of developing the skill and can now teach it step by step.

Dick Motta, 1971 NBA Coach of the Year, and a member of the Basketball Hall of Fame said, "I never played in an organized basketball game in my life (unless you count church ball as organized)."

The first NBA game Dick saw, he coached. He won over 900 professional games; the fifth most by any NBA coach ever.

More often than not, the mentor gains greater knowledge on how to teach the skill than the person he is working with.

Great coaches therefore have coaches. They mentor each other.

Most great coaches enjoy working with other coaches because it helps them refine their coaching abilities. As I said, coaches need coaches; mentors need mentors; great coaches need both.

My Dad was my first coach and mentor. No, he did not coach a little league team. He coached me in the sport called "work".

His favorite comment was, "Hard work is important but it's not the most important thing. How you work hard is more important than how hard you work."

At the risk of being repetitive, I repeat. *"How you work hard* is more important than *how hard you work."*

My Dad called this, "Smart Work."

Whether I was mending a fence, cleaning a ditch, stacking hay or taking the sheep to the pasture, Dad would watch me for a minute then he would ask, "Is there a smarter way to do that? A faster way?

A better way?"

There usually was. He would give me a chance to figure it out. If I was unable to figure it out by myself, he would work me through it. The reward of accomplishment made even mundane tasks seem worthwhile – and fun.

He showed me *how* to do "smart work"; how to discipline myself to the task at hand; how to stay on track as well as how to pace myself so I would not trail off at the end of a project.

Whenever I started something, he was there to encourage me and make sure I finished the job. He would always tell me, "It isn't how you start, it's how well you finish that counts."

He ingrained smart work into me so deeply that, even at the ripe old age of eighty, whenever a new task comes before me my first thought is, "What is the smartest way to accomplish this?"

It was my father who taught me the key: "Plan your work and work your plan." He said it, he meant it, and he practiced it – daily. It was his mantra and, with a very slight alteration, it became my mantra for coaching champions:

"Plan your race and race your plan."

Dad worked as a fireman and as a farmer. His shift as a fireman was 24 hours on, 48 hours off. We farmed together two days then he would be gone the next day. He expected me to accomplish as much when he was gone as I would if he were there.

He would lay out his plan for the day and we would follow it to the tee. Detailed planning was part of his smart work. The night before he would go off to be a fireman, he would tell me what needed to be accomplished the next day and expect me to come up with a plan for getting it done. The next morning, before he left for work, he would review my plan for the day.

Sometimes, after listening to my plan, he would grin and say, "If you follow that plan, Chick, you are in for a long day."

I would then take more time to think of more ways that I could work smart.

"Plan your race and race your plan" is good advice for athletes.

It is *great* advice for the race of life.

Like good fathers, good bosses can naturally become great coaches and mentors. Dr. Lionel Drechsel was the principal at Ben Lomond High School when I was hired on as a history teacher and first time track coach.

He could see the potential in this young, enthusiastic, pushy and sometimes out-of-control coach. During my first two years, I am pretty sure I got called into his office more times than any of the students. There were times when he could have – maybe even should have – put me on probation. But he never did.

Dr. Drechsel demonstrated the patience of Job in working with me; and by example showed me I needed more patience in working with my athletes – and to not fly off the handle so quick and so often.

He taught me to always look for the good first in my athletes and, when they did something wrong, spend less time criticizing them and more time teaching them how to do it better. He was more of a coach and mentor than a boss.

At the first high school state championship meet I attended as a coach, I watched the runners from South High School, Salt Lake City, dominate the hurdle races. They had three or four of the top six places in both races.

How could this be? How could one school be so outstanding in one area?

I decided to find out. The Utah High School Athletic Association conducted a coaching clinic that summer. The first thing I did when I got to the clinic was look up the South High School coach, Nate Long.

I followed Coach Long around like a puppy for three days, asking him every question I could think of about hurdling. Then I would go home at night and read more about hurdling so I would have more questions to ask him the next day.

He taught me a philosophy that shaped my coaching career.

Nate told me that while he does not always have the fastest kids in the state, he does have kids fast enough to be outstanding hurdlers if he teaches them good hurdling technique.

He always taught his best sprinters how to hurdle. "You can't get a college scholarship by placing fourth or fifth in the sprints at State," he said, "but you *can* get a scholarship by winning the hurdles."

Coach Long spent many winter hours working with his hurdlers in the hallways of South High School long after the other teachers and coaches had left for the day.

He showed me how to break the hurdle technique down into parts and how to teach each part to the athletes. He taught me the value and importance of repetition in coaching. Coach Long not only coached at South High School, he also coached me.

It took me two years to apply his ideas and become proficient at coaching the hurdles, but I stuck to it. Coach Long's South High and my Ben Lomond High School athletes dominated the hurdles in the state of Utah for the next eight years.

By the way, neither Coach Long nor I ever ran any type of a hurdle race in our life.

When Wade Bell was being recruited by the University of Oregon, I had the opportunity to get acquainted with Bill Bowerman, one who coached more sub four-minute milers than any coach in the United States. This outstanding distant coach was always willing to share his knowledge. In fact, he gave Wade permission to send me all of Wade's workouts.

I would call Coach Bowerman and he would explain to me what the purpose of the particular workout was and how it should help and develop Wade. In turn, I would tell him what my workouts were for my runners and he would offer suggestions on how I might improve them.

Coach Bowerman was indeed a coach's coach.

For the next twenty years, Coach Bowerman was a mentor and friend. He enhanced my knowledge about track & field and taught me many ways to improve my coaching techniques.

Coach Bowerman inspired me to always pay attention to coaches in other sports and see what techniques they were using that could be adapted to coaching track.

Bowerman began his career as a football coach. He also coached swimming for a while. When he started to coach distance runners he used the interval training he had learned in coaching swimming to help his runners develop sub four minute mile capabilities.

Ten years later most of the track coaches in the United States were copying Bowerman's ideas – the ideas that came from a swimming coach. Coach Bowerman always stated that he could learn from anyone that was teaching good technique – and transfer what and how he learned to any other discipline or event.

When Henry Marsh, a BYU graduate and Olympian went to the University of Oregon to work on his law degree, Bowerman became his coach. Henry's steeplechase times improved dramatically under Bowerman's tutelage, and he set the American Record in the event.

When Henry moved back to Utah, Bill suggested he should do his workouts with me at Weber because I understood his methods and could supplement his coaching. Henry would get his workout plans from Coach Bowerman. We would adapt the workouts to our altitude in Utah.

After twenty years of being mentored by Coach Bowerman, the workouts that I was putting Farley Gerber through were very close to what Bowerman wanted Henry to do. After a while Henry started to do Farley's workouts, they worked together for three years. During that time, Farley set the American Collegiate record in the Steeplechase and Henry broke his own American record in the Steeplechase.

That is what happens when one outstanding coach is willing to coach another coach.

When I first met Coach Martin Smith, he was already a very successful distance and cross country coach at the University of Wisconsin. At that time, he was the only NCAA cross country coach that had won an NCAA championship, coaching *both* a men's and a women's team.

He knew about our success at Weber and wanted to find out the reason for our success. As great as a coach as he was, he wanted to be mentored in the Steeplechase. That was great for me because he could teach me a lot about cross country and the 5K and 10K races in return.

Although Martin Smith had been coaching for over ten years he had a thirst for knowledge to add another distant event to his repertoire. Coach Smith and I spent hours talking about our specialties in the distant events. Sometimes we stayed up all night learning from each other.

On a couple of occasions, he flew out personally to see how we were coaching the Steeple and to help me with my distance runners. In return, I went to the University of Wisconsin to better understand the techniques he was using with his 5K and 10K runners and help him with his steeplechasers.

We became each other's coaches. We both benefited greatly from our relationship. I got more All Americans in the 5K and 10K races and he coached two NCAA Champions in the steeplechase!

In 1991, we relied on each other's expertise to develop strategies that helped our cross country teams place well in the NCAA Cross Country Championships.[13]

Coaches need mentors. Mentors need coaches. Great coaches continuously seek out ways to enhance the best in those they coach and instill in them the habit of exceeding their personal best in business, at home, in life – for the rest of their lives.

Drechsel, Bowerman, Long, Smith – and my dad. Great coaches improve themselves as they inspire greatness in others.

---

13   See chapter eight.

About the Author

USA Track and Field Hall of Fame and Olympic Coach, Chick Hislop has been selected for many honors including Ben Lomond High School Hall of Fame; Weber State University Hall of Fame; Utah Sports Hall of Fame; United States Track Coaches Hall of Fame; NCAA Cross-Country National Coach of the Year.

He has coached the American Record holder in the Steeplechase, forty-six All-American track athletes and a Masters Track & Field World Record holder. Coach Hislop feels that his most important accomplishment is inspiring athletes to constantly improve their personal best in athletics and in life as well as being true team players.

As of this printing, Coach has been married fifty-nine years to his wonderfully supportive wife, Dianne. He is proud papa to five children, Elynn, Lance, Jill, Chris, Kim – all graduates of Weber State University – and seventeen grandchildren (so far).

About the Editor

Why would we write "about the editor"? Because he deserves it. Thomas Cantrell is known for his ability to hear what authors want to say and help them say it the way they really mean to say it. That is what a "creative editor" does. He is a presenter of ideas that challenge the standard of common thought; and he gives his ideas away as fast as they come to him.

Author and speaker in his own right, his greatest calling, however, is to empower others to change the world by saying the right thing at the right time to the right people in the right way.